PROFIT

OVER
PRODUCTION

UNDERSTAND DENTAL BUSINESS AND CHOOSE YOUR PRACTICE DESTINY

Fleur-de-Lis Publishing
© 2023 by Julie C. Woods, DDS, MS
Published 2023
Printed in the United States of America

10 9 8 7 6 5 4 3
ISBN: 979-8-9875402-1-3 (paperback)
ISBN: 979-8-9875402-6-8 (e-book)
ISBN: 979-8-9875402-4-4 (audiobook)

Subjects: 1. Dental business—profit.
2. Dental business—cash management and accounting.
3. Dental business—ideal schedule.
4. Dental business—employment acquisition and retention.

Disclaimer: The information contained in this book is
for information purposes only and is not intended to
take the place of in-person professional guidance.
Books may be purchased in bulk for educational or business use.
Please contact your local bookseller or julie@drjuliewoods.com.

Edited by AJ Harper and Zoë Bird
Proofread by Ellen E. Horn
Typeset by Choi Messer
Cover design by Choi Messer
Cover photos by Jennifer Goetz

For Rachel

CONTENTS

INTRODUCTION

ONE EVENING WHILE I WAS sitting at our dining room table, frantically typing chapters to submit to my editor, the following conversation ensued with my teenage daughter. She was a sophomore in high school at the time and considering becoming a dentist.

Rachel asked, "Mom, why are you writing a book? What's it even about? Is it even going to sell?"

"Rachel, do you really think I would write a book that I didn't believe would sell? That I would spend this much time and energy if I didn't think this book would help someone?"

"Well, you're a dentist. You're *not* an author. You don't even know how to write!"

Whoa! While I am sure my high school English teacher would agree about my writing capabilities, realizing that my daughter thought my abilities were limited to my job title caught me off guard. To her credit, I am a dentist. Actually, I am a periodontist. I have worked in private practice since completing my periodontal residency at Baylor College of Dentistry in 2004 and have owned my practice for more than seventeen years. And at the time of this conversation, I *was* technically a published author, as my thesis project can be found in the 2005 *Journal of Periodontology*,[1] but I didn't mention that to her.

"Just because I'm a dentist doesn't mean I don't know how to write," I said.

"Mom," she replied with complete disdain, "only people who go to college to learn to write, write books. What is your book even about?"

"Do you really want to know?"

"Yes."

"This book is for dentists who are frustrated because they want to have a successful dental practice but think the only way to do that is to produce more. Or, in other words, do more dentistry. They don't realize that producing more does not always mean making more money and that it certainly doesn't guarantee they will have a successful practice."

"Dentists are smart," Rachel said. "They make a lot of money. Why doesn't it work for them to just see more patients or do more dentistry?"

"Well, most dentists have only been taught to focus on production and collections, or the money that comes in. Many don't understand as much about the money going out."

"Isn't that common sense? Don't they understand that, as business owners, they can't spend more than they bring in?"

"Think back to what Mr. Thomas taught you in eighth grade," I said. "How only about 40% of Americans could cover a $1,000 emergency. Dentists are *just* people. We had very little instruction about the business side of owning a practice when we were in dental school."

Mr. Thomas was Rachel's eighth-grade math teacher and an avid fan of Dave Ramsey, so he sprinkled many principles from Ramsey's book *The Total Money Makeover*[2] into his teaching. Since Mr. Thomas was also one of the Financial Peace University (FPU) coordinators who volunteered to lead participants through Ramsey's Financial Peace program, Rachel had learned more about cash management in eighth grade than I had before graduating from dental school.

I was so happy that Mr. Thomas introduced some practical concepts, like how making lots of money doesn't mean you have lots of money. His students learned, for example, how their paychecks would not equal the number of hours worked multiplied by their hourly rate.

I thought it was telling that my daughter could not fathom dentists not understanding business basics or how to handle money. However, as a dentist who once had major financial woes of my own, I know this scenario is all too common.

DENTISTRY'S DIRTY LITTLE SECRET

In 2020, DENTISTS HAD TO deal with COVID-19, a "suggested" shutdown of services, and supply issues. The Great Resignation followed. While global pandemics are known to wreak havoc, I certainly did not expect this one to threaten dental practice viability on the scale that it did. Social media became a place for us to "meet" even when forced to isolate, and there I witnessed—and felt—the pressure to survive more than ever. It became evident that without government assistance, many dentists would no longer be able to serve their patients or communities.

Dental service organizations (DSOs) and private equity firms used the uncertainty to their advantage and were able to take over a greater share of dental practice ownership. While I was alarmed at how quickly things were changing within the industry, from one practice owner to another, I totally understood. Way before COVID-19 brought its unique set of challenges, I was exhausted, struggling with physical ailments, and unable to understand how to correct my "money" problem. Being a solo practitioner was far harder than I'd imagined it would be and not nearly as glamorous. I was desperate and needed help. I didn't even know where to begin. All I knew for certain was that producing more dentistry wasn't the answer.

A microscopic virus exposed dentistry's dirty little secret: Dentists lack business knowledge.

DENTISTS LACK BUSINESS KNOWLEDGE. THEY WENT TO DENTAL SCHOOL TO LEARN DENTISTRY.

Specifically, many dentists don't know how to talk about or deal with money and don't want to. I know I didn't, at first. Dentists go to dental school to become dentists, and figure the rest will sort itself out (I thought that too until I had to think differently). Unfortunately, that simply isn't true.

My colleagues were in crisis mode back in 2020, struggling to maintain their businesses. I knew that I had the expertise to help them navigate financial uncertainty. I had turned my business around by drastically reducing my overhead costs and increasing profitability. I enjoyed talking about money, numbers, and grants. While some dentists focused on the infection control side of surviving the pandemic, I decided to focus on helping other dentists understand the nuances of the Paycheck Protection Program (PPP) loans as well as the other grants that became available. I upped my knowledge of cash management by completing my certification as a Profit First Professional (PFP). That allowed me to leverage the resources of a group of international PFPs, many of whom come from an accounting, banking, or business background. If there was a question I couldn't readily answer on my own, I had over 600 experts to fall back on, including the author of *Profit First*, Mike Michalowicz.[3]

I have since helped hundreds of dentists evaluate their practice numbers and talked with them about how their business financial insecurities bleed into other practice or personal issues with no direct links to finances. Some of them were interviewed for this book, and to protect their privacy, some names have been changed.

After I've helped them build their confidence and "armed" them with the data to have conversations with their bankers, they have been able to pay off student and business loans or refinance their current business loans with better terms and lower rates. I regularly receive messages from excited clients who tell me they've just paid cash for a new piece of equipment or their teenager's car. I have even had dentists thank me for making sure they had enough cash on hand when it was time to pay the IRS. Most importantly, through our work together, dentists have increased their profitability *without having to produce more*, work more days, or see more patients.

THE BOOK *WE* NEED

THE NOVELIST TONI MORRISON IS often quoted as saying, "If there is a book that you want to read, but it hasn't been written yet, then you must write it."[4] The book you currently hold is the one I desperately *needed* when I found my practice was in financial trouble. It would have been extremely helpful during my early years of practice ownership.

I never imagined I would write a book, much less a prescriptive nonfiction book. But when I started sharing more about my practice and financial struggles, I received numerous requests for a book that other dentists could reference. Some asked for some version of "Accounting for Dentists," others for something along the lines of "Profit First for Dummies." The overwhelming need of so many colleagues sparked the inspiration for this book. I began to pursue writing a "good" book that would help readers transform their dental practices and, more importantly, their lives.

I'm on a mission to bust the myth that all you need to do is "produce more" to be successful, stable, and happy. You and I can no longer be "just dentists" who don't understand business. We must learn to think and act like a dental CEO, or what I like to refer to as the "dentist officer in charge (DOC)," to maintain a sustainably profitable business.

I want to stop for a minute and share how I came up with this term. I wanted a title that was unique to those of us who are both dentists *and* the head honchos, bosses, and owners of our practices, a term that gave weight to all the aspects that I believe encompass a successful dentist and practice owner. *And* I wanted it to be easy for everyone to remember. The list of titles I threw out includes "dental business owner," "dental financial officer," and "chief dental officer." However, all of those could apply to non-dentists acting in those roles, while I wanted to celebrate and emphasize the fact that being the actual *dentist* within the practice is a valuable strength. I was super excited that the acronym wasn't going to be something unusable, like "DIC." On the other hand, it's a pet peeve of mine when patients call me "Doc" and I don't want anyone to think I am talking down to them. So please note, the way I *say* the acronym for dentist officer in charge is "D-O-C," much like you or I would pronounce CEO as "C-E-O." Get it? Got it? Okay, good. Now, where was I? Oh yes, thinking like a DOC and not "just" a dentist.

Even if many of our values do not align with dental service organizations (DSOs), we must start treating our practices as businesses, something DSOs are far better at doing. That said, I don't want anyone to think that I wrote this book to teach you how to make the most money. While I do plan to teach you better ways to be profitable so that you no longer have to stay on the production line, drilling and filling on the fast track to burnout, my intention in doing so is to help you create enough financial security to figure out if you even care that much about producing one million or two million dollars—or if you just think you *have to* because that's what you *believe* "everyone else" is doing.

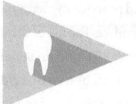

MONEY MANAGEMENT ALONE WON'T BRING SUCCESS OR HAPPINESS.

Money management alone won't bring success or happiness; however, the financial security derived from owning a sustainably profitable dental practice *will* allow you the time and mental bandwidth to figure out how to live the life you want. I believe that if you learn better ways to work smarter, not harder, you can then determine if you are actually practicing the way you want to, if you want to work more or expand, or if you even want to be a dentist.

I hope that in reading about my own experiences and financial struggles, as well as the major wins that have come since I learned to think like a DOC, you will be inspired to share more openly about the good and bad, the ups and downs of owning a dental office. Collaboration and working as a "team" to navigate cash and business management will help us conquer our limitations and become profitable—what I like to refer to as summiting Profit Mountain.

PROFIT MOUNTAIN:

An imaginary elevation along the path of life that is larger and steeper than a hill and can block forward progression. Upon summiting this mountain, climbers will feel more secure in their financial footing, allowing them to prepare for future adventures with confidence.

By doing it together, we can go faster and with fewer missteps, allowing us the time and mental bandwidth to figure out how we *want* to practice when we are no longer financially bound to "produce more."

I hope that if we do a better job mentoring each other and passing on needed information to newer dentists now, by the time my daughter finishes dental school, she will be able to enter private practice and work on patients without *having to* work for a DSO or be manipulated by corporate greed due to her own financial and business insecurities. I do not want her to feel so burdened by student debt that she thinks that's her only option. I hope she can find a practice she wants to purchase or dares to start the practice she envisions. I don't want her to feel like she must accept insurance reimbursements that continue to decline despite the rising costs of doing business. Burnout should be something she can avoid altogether because she will know not to work herself to death. Like most parents, I want my daughter to have the best opportunity to succeed.

All my hopes and wishes coming true start with you. It's time to conquer whatever lies in your path, to begin the arduous climb up Profit Mountain. Thankfully, I have already gathered much of the equipment, tools, and expertise you will need. As you read along, imagine me right beside you on this journey. It's imperative that we reach the summit. The future of private dental practices is dependent on our success. Let's blaze this trail together so that all dentists have the opportunity to succeed and live the lives they want!

A NOTE
ABOUT FOR WHOM THIS BOOK IS INTENDED

IF YOU CONSIDER YOURSELF A savvy entrepreneur or businessperson and you are as puzzled as my teenager who wondered, "How is it possible that dentists don't know their numbers or how to handle day-to-day operations?" If so, this book is *not* for you. If you're one of the people on social media who constantly post or comment about your bazillion-dollar practice or your multiple offices, this book is *not* for you. If you own several luxury cars and a home that could be featured on TV as well as a vacation home, you definitely need to put the book down.

However, if you find yourself drowning in debt while questioning why on earth you went through all the trouble of becoming a dentist, you're holding the right book. If you are wondering how any dentist could afford a second home while you can barely make the mortgage payment on your primary residence, you are holding the book that was written for you. It was never in my five- or ten-year plan to write a book. I wrote it because dentists asked me to. In fact, they begged. They wanted a reference resource and have been too afraid to ask for help elsewhere.

So many dentists who are both clients and friends talk to me about their insecurities and questions about running a business. Many think they're the only ones with these problems. Dentists have felt isolated and alone for many years. The advent of social media groups seemed to be a great solution to this problem, as they offered a place for dentists to connect and learn from each other. No one had to feel alone anymore. Sadly, it all backfired. Those who participate the most get the most attention. Many of the loudest are the dentists who claim to have all their shit figured out. Not only are they masters of the clinical side of dentistry—just look at their amazing photos— they are also business gurus. They never suffer burnout or have team problems. Patients are always super appreciative, and ready to pay more for the amazing quality of their work. Insurance issues? None. These dental gods are all fee-for-service and do not even consider helping patients who have the nerve to choose in-network dentists that are contracted with their employers' insurance companies.

The dentists that fall short of these astronomical benchmarks tend to feel *more* intimidated than before. They become quieter. Embarrassed. Afraid to ask questions, even amongst "friends." In a time when dentists should feel more supported and less alone, they feel like imposters, like they don't measure up to their peers, and like they have no one to ask for advice since it is expected that they already know how to do "all the things."

This culture, of dentists boasting of success and pretending life in dentistry is always grand, is toxic. Those who are unwilling to share the tough realities are certainly not helping their colleagues or future dentists heading into the workforce. Dentists who are primarily concerned with dominating their competition and unwilling to share any secrets of their success prove just how destructive operating from a scarcity mindset can be.

The dentists for whom I wrote this book are willing to increase their business knowledge, learn from others, improve their skills, and question the old way of doing things. They do not think they have it all figured out, nor do they boast of their success or happiness. They want to work together to make things better. In fact, many of the dentists I asked to give me feedback on the first draft of my manuscript told me they thought this book should be shared with their office managers and accountants. One of those readers told me to make sure dentists know that, while the tax tips included are geared toward dealing with the U.S. tax code, most of the other information applies to dentists practicing outside of the U.S.

If you're a dentist who wants to better your practice life by learning how to understand the business of dentistry, keep reading: You will learn that *and* how to practice the way you want, and can then help others do the same. You will be a true trailblazer, leading the way for the next generation of dentists so they, too, have the opportunity to become successful entrepreneurs.

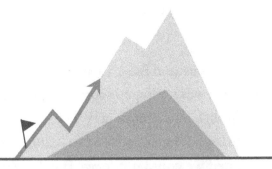

CHAPTER 1
BURNED OUT AND BROKE

RUSHING OUT OF MY OFFICE after seeing my morning patients, I headed to McDonald's for a double cheeseburger Happy Meal®. I was anything but happy. I tried to ignore my nausea long enough to choke down my food as tears dropped onto the yellow wrapper. This had become my routine.

It was the end of 2017, the hardest year I'd experienced since I started private practice in 2004. I was "burned out," but I didn't really even know what that meant. I dreaded Sunday evenings, going to work, and even eating lunch in the office. I no longer had the energy or mental bandwidth to interact with my team or put up a good front. Many afternoons, I ended up in tears. My daughter Rachel, a preteen at the time, even asked my husband if I was okay. Having dealt with depression off and on since losing my sister in a car accident over Labor Day weekend of 1990, I wondered if I was slipping into clinical depression. I was seeing a counselor and taking antidepressants, but nothing seemed to help.

That spring, my husband Brad, a general and trauma surgeon at a local hospital, was finding his current position untenable and on the verge of his own burnout. We had been married just short of two years, but he understood that due to my practice and my daughter, we could not leave Topeka, Kansas. One week, he felt so exhausted, frustrated, and discouraged that he printed out his resignation letter "just in case" and carried it with him to work. Before the week was over, he had turned in his notice and was soon to be unemployed.

I was supportive as Brad began actively pursuing job leads and felt somewhat relieved when he was offered a job at one of the hospitals in the Kansas City area, a little over an hour from our home in Topeka. I had no idea how much resentment would slowly start to build as he began his new job and spent half his time away from us. Now we had two mortgages to pay, since he had to be within twenty minutes of the hospital when he was on call and we were at the stage of life where we did not want to rent an apartment. The pressure for me to produce more at my office only intensified. I became more anxious. More overwhelmed.

However, I did what was necessary and worked more. Produced more. We only took the vacations we already had scheduled. Even though I was miserable at work and truly felt like I was on a hamster wheel I couldn't hop out of, I kept at it. I didn't know what else to do.

As the year wound down, I knew I had done what I set out to do. Production was up, as were our collections. So why was there no money in the bank? All the once-a-year bills were piling up and our Christmas luncheon was days away. Since I purchased the practice in 2006, I have passed out crisp new hundred-dollar bills like a total baller at the end of the luncheon. I'm not really that cool, but it was the highlight of the year for my crew. (Before anyone gets too hung up on these bonuses being actual cash, I paid what was owed to the IRS as the bonuses were recorded as part of staff payroll. The bonuses have never been tied to production or collections. I have always considered them a gesture of goodwill and figured them into my staff's annual salaries.)

I barely had enough money to cover a round of burgers at McDonald's, much less take my crew to our normal lunch and pay them. There was not enough money in the bank. I could not make sense of where the money had gone.

Sitting in the car, crying into my cheeseburger, I knew there was only one option. I had to go home and ask Brad if we could put some of our own money back into the business. I could not let my team down. They were counting on that money and would never have believed we didn't have it. Maybe you have never been so desperate as to settle for the comfort of fast food, but I'm guessing you have gone home, poured a generous serving of wine—in your "because patients" glass—and ruminated over the frustrations of owning a dental office. Or, if you are way healthier than I am, maybe you've gone home and ridden your Peloton to the point of fatigue, allowing your mind to clear. Instead of a stomachache or headache, you got to enjoy the rush of serotonin.

I'm sure that putting caffeine, burgers, and wine on repeat didn't do my body any favors. However, I was able to get up each morning, see all the patients on the schedule that December, and enjoy our annual luncheon and Secret Sock exchange.

That Christmas break, I began reading *Profit First* by Mike Michalowicz at the urging of my bookkeeper. She was not exactly sure what the issue was with my practice, but she knew there was a major problem with cash flow and expenses despite our levels of production and collections.

As I sat in front of our fireplace reading, I felt like Mike was describing me and *my* "cash-eating monster" of a dental practice. I began to make plans for implementing the system. And then, much like many dentists I talk to now, I became overwhelmed with the process and my enthusiasm began to dwindle. Soon, I was off on our annual trip to the Cayman Islands.

While we were there, my self-proclaimed office manager put up one of those vague Facebook posts about being unappreciated. I immediately began texting the remainder of my team and quizzing them, asking if that post was directed at me. I also asked if they felt the same way. I was disappointed, especially since Brad and I had put our own money back into the business to cover all their Christmas cash. It was the day before we were to leave the Cayman Islands and I did not want to return to my practice. I could not finish dinner, I felt so sick. This was another sign that all was not well within the walls of my dental office.

When I got back, the bookkeeper began working on an expense analysis, looking at every single item purchased within a certain time frame to see if it was necessary or not. She quickly ascertained that the "office supplies" were more than double what they should be. After asking for every invoice and every purchase made, my bookkeeper found evidence that the office manager—let's call her "Stacie"—had ordered personal items through our business Quill account. She even had the audacity to have some of the orders sent to her home address. When I investigated Stacie's payroll hours, I found that she had also abused her permission to fix timesheet mistakes. She had padded her hours for months, including the day of the Christmas luncheon. I will never forget the day I terminated her employment, nor the months following when I felt so duped. We all did. The rest of us had been working relentlessly while she took more than her fair share. We are still using up some of the Post-its she ordered four years ago so that she could get a free crockpot with her purchase.

Maybe you have never lost control of your practice to the point of theft, but if you have any kind of expense problem, you might find yourself in a similar predicament, wondering why there seems to be nothing to show for all your hard work. As you keep producing more and earning the same, you and your team will start to show signs of burnout.

Don't do what I did. Don't read this book and think, *Yeah, I should do that* and then go on vacation. If you keep on focusing on production, your viewpoint will be stuck at the level of the mouth and you will most likely miss what is happening to your cash and profits. You might not discover that your business is unhealthy until it's on life support and you find yourself in a financial hole that is difficult to climb out of.

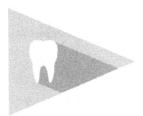

PRODUCING MORE
DOES NOT GUARANTEE
THAT YOU WILL MAKE
MORE MONEY.

We must get the word out to our colleagues that producing more *no longer* guarantees profitability. This is especially true now that insurance companies are lowering reimbursement rates *and* the costs of business are climbing. As dentists, we can no longer rely on our skills as practitioners to ensure our success. Even though we did not receive much (if any) business training in school, we must realize that a practice *is* a business. *All businesses must be profitable to be sustainable.* We have to think and act like business CEOs or DOCs (dentist officers in charge) to ensure profitability.

Trust me, I didn't want to act like a CEO, be the DOC, or learn anything about the business, but I was out of options. I didn't have a choice. I'm hoping this book reaches your hands while you still have options, and that you choose to learn more about business so you can live the life you envisioned without the heartache or burnout I had to muddle through.

PRODUCING MORE DOES NOT EQUATE TO EARNING MORE

I ALREADY MENTIONED THAT WHEN I was at the height of my production and collections, I still wasn't taking home more money; nor was there any extra money in the bank. In fact, there was less cash in the business than ever, and I was forced to put some of my own money back into the business. Clearly, "dental experts" had left an important part of the equation out of their "produce more, earn more" mantra.

I had a colleague reach out to me after listening to one of my podcast interviews, in which I revealed that my expense percentage was in the eighties during that period.[5] Her message read, "I was thinking, 'Mine is definitely not as bad as that,' but really, going through the numbers today, it's pretty damn close. I was disheartened to discover that with my debt payments included, my profit is essentially zero and my expenses are at 79%, which is definitely not where I thought they were." I get messages like this all the time. All. The. Time. Many dentists don't know the percentage of collections that they spend on their expenses.

In full transparency, I admit that I had no idea how much I was spending back then either. Nor did I know how much I was or should be spending on expenses like staff, dental supplies, rent, utilities, etc. My overhead was over 84%! For every dollar we collected, I took home less than sixteen cents. The harsh reality is that I had a negative profit. Who even knew that was a thing? No wonder I was miserable.

It was time to get my *Profit First* book off the shelf and reread it. In it, Mike outlines a system that guarantees profitability starting from the first day of implementation. I opened the bank accounts he suggested and began working the system early in 2018. I have since paid off all my business and school loan debt (early), invested or utilized profit sharing in my 401(k) as desired, and maintained my take-home pay without having to work more. Overhead is down over 40% despite the decrease in collections and the rising costs of doing business that have resulted from the pandemic, the Great Resignation, and the inflation that followed. My periodontal practice is viable and I'm still the sole practitioner.

BRINGING IN MILLIONS DOESN'T MEAN YOU CAN MAKE PAYROLL

WHEN I FIRST MET WITH "Dr. Reynolds" to review her financials over Zoom, she excitedly told me, "You will have to share with Chris that my team and I are all set to meet our two-million-dollar production goal this year." The Chris she referred to is Chris Sands, a fellow PFP, co-owner of Pro-Fi 20/20 Dental CPAs, and an Accredited Wealth Management Advisor (AWMA).

After seeing a YouTube video in which Chris interviewed me about my journey from burned-out practice owner to "The Profit First Dentist," Dr. Reynolds reached out to me to see if I would be willing to evaluate her current financial situation.[6] She had worked with Chris years prior, before he co-founded Pro-Fi 20/20, to implement a similar cash management system in which she allocated money to multiple accounts. When there was not enough money to cover the continuing education (CE) trips and new equipment she wanted to buy, she abandoned the system.

Dr. Reynolds is a general dentist in Texas. She has been practicing dentistry for over twenty-five years. After we swapped a few Texas dental school stories, she enthusiastically explained how glad she was to meet so that she could share her big news.

"Julie, we have been working toward this two-million-dollar goal for years. It has always felt out of reach."

She thought that if they hit that production goal, she and her associate would not only feel successful, but she would also be a more profitable practice owner. Sadly, that was not the case. I dreaded sharing my findings with her.

When I evaluated Dr. Reynolds's financial reports to determine how much she was spending on staff, rent, debt payments, and other big expenses, I found that her overhead was over 100%. That meant more money was leaving her practice than was coming in from patient collections. Initially, I thought I must have made a mistake. Surely she was not that short on cash in the bank. I must have miscalculated. I had just seen a post on Instagram that showed photos of her and a couple of staff members attending a CE event in Las Vegas.

While she and I sat face to face (over our computers) to discuss my findings, I asked her, "Michelle, is it possible for you to log in into your bank account while we are on our Zoom? I would like to know exactly how much cash you have in your bank accounts. Your balance sheet is showing negative amounts in the accounts. That usually means that the bookkeeping is not current."

"Sure, give me just a minute. Okay, the total for the business is $7,265.00."

"Is that the total of all the accounts, Michelle? Your balance sheet shows that you have four separate accounts."

"Yes, that's all of them. The total balance is *only* that high because I put some of my own money back into the business to cover payroll for Monday."

I was shocked. Here was a dentist who thought that reaching her office's annual production goal of two million dollars was going to make her successful. She also assumed that this would make her more profitable. Her story was eerily similar to my own, with one key difference: She was not in the least bit concerned about putting her own money back into the business to cover payroll. She just said, "it's *only* that high"—as if less than $10,000 for a dental practice is *high*. It was quite obvious to me, by the way she smiled and told me stories from her recent trip to Vegas, that she had no idea of the gravity of the situation. Her business was failing, and she didn't even know it.

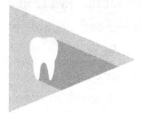

PRODUCING TWO MILLION DOLLARS A YEAR DOESN'T MEAN YOU CAN COVER PAYROLL.

I explained that more money was leaving the practice than she was bringing in and that it appeared she was spending roughly 50% of collections on staff expenses. *Double what she should be spending.*

Dr. Reynolds shrugged and said, "I've always thought of my staff as my children."

As I wrapped up the call, I confirmed that she still wanted me to share my findings, and her big news about production, with Chris.

I remember how dejected I felt when I got off that Zoom call. This was a dentist who had been practicing since 1988. She and her team were indeed getting close to making their two-million-dollar production goal, but her overhead was over 100% and her income statements consistently showed losses.

She planned to retire within the next few years and there were already talks in the works for her associate to buy the practice.

I frantically texted Chris, asking if he remembered working with Dr. Reynolds. He did. I let him know that she had asked me to share her news and given me permission to share my findings. We agreed that she was in trouble. He confirmed one of my fears, that there was not enough cash flow for the associate to purchase the business. No banker would be willing to cover such a risky loan. Dr. Reynolds was going to have refocus her efforts on working *on* the business, not just helping to produce more dentistry. She had to quit thinking of her staff as her children. She was running a business. She had to start thinking of herself as a DOC, not just the generous mom of the practice.

Dr. Reynolds is not alone in thinking that more production means more money. I too used to think that producing more dentistry was the answer to all my practice problems.

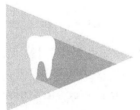

MORE PRODUCTION DOES NOT ENSURE MORE PROFIT OR EQUATE TO SUCCESS.

After I implemented Profit First in my own practice, it became all too evident to me that, sometimes, production growth just means an increase in expenses and more money going out, not more profit. So, in addition to tracking production and collections, I paid closer attention to how much money left the practice and where it went. I researched the industry averages for expenses and figured out where mine were too high. I made difficult decisions about the staff. I opened additional bank accounts and started moving money as outlined in *Profit First*. Soon, I was out of the financial hole and starting my hike up Profit Mountain.

I refused to keep doing the same thing—producing more—while expecting a different outcome. Isn't that the definition of insanity?[7] I needed a new perspective. I knew I couldn't keep my focus only on the mouth. I had to look beyond the operatory, beyond the practice. Even though I felt like I could barely see a way out of the financial pit I was in, I began to feel some hope. I started envisioning a better life. One where I wasn't stuck at work.

WHAT IT TAKES TO HAVE A SUCCESSFUL PRACTICE *AND* LIVE THE WAY YOU WANT

REMEMBER THE MESSAGE I MENTIONED earlier, from the dentist who was surprised to discover that her expenses were as bad as mine? Well, you will be glad to know that while she was disheartened, she too felt hopeful that she could "turn [her practice] around and start moving in the right direction." I responded quickly, reassuring her that she could indeed turn her practice around because she was brave enough to look at her numbers. I will tell you the same thing: **It's not too late to change your practice destiny**. Even if you have sold a practice to a DSO or are practicing but unsure you even want to be a dentist, don't lose hope. Frankly, as long as you are alive, it will never be too late.

I wrote this book so you don't have to work so hard that you burn out and consider leaving dentistry. There is no need for you to suffer unnecessarily. You can use my experience as proof that you must do things differently.

You will learn how to conduct your own "Limited Financial Exam" to correctly diagnose any financial ailments your practice might be suffering. This tool was inspired by the Instant Assessment in *Profit First,* but I have tailored it specifically to our professional needs. Information obtained from your exam will give you the starting point to begin working *on,* not just *in,* your practice and learning how to think like a DOC. By the time you finish reading this book, you will understand what leads to a successful dental practice without having to kill yourself in the process. You will learn to practice and live the way you want.

But first, you will have to gear up for a tough climb. At times, you may feel like you have been climbing for days or had to bushwhack your way to a new path. If you use this book as a guide, it will help you stay on the easiest, shortest, and safest path to the peak.

I plan to act as your trail angel—yes, that's a real thing—to keep you from inadvertently stumbling over a deadfall, help you check your gear, and make sure you have what you need. I will celebrate with you as you blaze your trail up Profit Mountain. You've already planted your first trailblazer flag by completing this chapter.

Don't get overwhelmed.

Keep your eyes on the path before you and take one step at a time.

Don't give up.

Keep hope alive.

You will make progress until you confidently say, "I did it! I summited Profit Mountain."

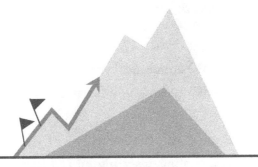

CHAPTER 2
MOVE FORWARD–DON'T STOP
BEFORE YOU START

THINK BACK OVER THE LAST few years and mentally list your favorite continuing education (CE) courses. I am certain that you had to struggle to sit still and pay attention in some of those classes. You impatiently tapped your feet, wishing the speaker would finish a little ahead of schedule and announce the verification code for credit so you could meet your friends at the bar or head to the pool—or, if you're like me, back to your room for a quiet afternoon reading a non-dental book.

I am also quite certain that you have attended courses taught by a friend or mentor, or one of the dental gurus you follow on social media or read about in dental literature. Perhaps it was on sleep apnea and airway. Maybe it was on cosmetic dentistry or Invisalign. If you are a periodontist or surgeon, it could have been a deep dive into complex cases involving implants and fixed hybrid dentures. Do you have your favorite in mind? Can you picture the city where you got to see the well-known speaker? Can you remember who was with you? A friend or colleague? Your clinical team? When you got home, did you implement anything you learned? What changed in your practice?

I don't know about you, but I can say with confidence that I have listened to motivating, inspiring, and educational speakers. I have spent a fair amount of money on consultants, courses, and travel, and paid for my team to go with me. I have sent them to courses without me. We have all come back excited and ready to transform some aspect of the practice, whether by offering a better patient experience or doing a better job presenting treatment options. We have changed and improved some of our systems. For example, in one course, my whole team learned the intricacies of dental implants, the costs to the patient, and the length of treatment time for a single tooth replacement versus full arch extractions followed by implants and a fixed hybrid denture. We all became comfortable speaking with patients about their options and the various costs involved. As a result, we saw a marked increase in our complex implant cases.

For every example I have about systems we changed or improved, there are probably five other systems, processes, or new methods that we didn't even try to implement because we thought we didn't have the right kind of patients for them to work or that our team didn't have the right skills or knowledge to pull them off. Many times, the fault was all mine; I didn't have the time to do one more thing because I was too busy trying to keep up with my production goals. That was when I still thought more production would lead to more money and success. I was wrong.

For things to change, you must change what you have been doing.

In this chapter, I will share the three most common reasons why you may not implement what you learn in this book. I want you to face these reasons head-on so you finish reading the book and use it as a guide to making changes within your practice.

Throughout the book, there are tasks I ask you to do, or questions I want you to answer, that can be completed or addressed in less than two minutes. These are denoted by a toothbrush symbol to indicate that they can be done in less time than it takes to brush your teeth. For tasks that take about as long as a periodontal maintenance appointment or a cutting a crown prep, I have used the tooth symbol so you know they will take a little longer than brushing your teeth but still less than an hour. If it will take more than an hour for you to complete a task, *or* if it will take even more time to see or feel a result, I use a clock symbol so you know it will take a little longer.

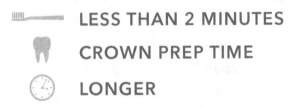

Figure 2.1: Time Symbol Key

Implementation of any new system can seem daunting when results are not immediately realized. As your trail angel, I plan to offer the encouragement you need to keep going even when those around you don't think the change is worth it, or you feel entrenched in an old mindset. Remember, doing the same thing over and over and expecting a different result is the definition of insanity. *Old-school thinking is not serving you anymore.* You will learn a different way, and I will make it as straightforward as possible for you to implement the systems. By the end of this book, you will have begun to transform your practice into one that is both more profitable and more enjoyable.

REASONS YOU MAY NOT CHANGE: LACK OF TIME

"I don't have time to learn about the business side of dentistry or make any changes."

Most dentists already work more days and hours than they want to, and are worried that if they aren't spending every hour at the office doing actual dentistry, they will not make enough money and the practice will fail. I know I certainly thought that. From the moment the former doctor retired and I became the sole periodontist and practice owner, I felt obligated to spend my practice time seeing patients. I worried that I might lose patients or referrals if I was not open to handling emergencies or seeing patients when it was convenient for them to visit our office. I thought that to be able to pay my business loan and cover rent, payroll, and all the other bills, I had to keep production up. Plus, I didn't think it was fair to take too many days off when the rest of my team depended on those hours to provide them enough take-home pay.

For close to seven years, I did not take more than a long weekend away from the office. The only reason I took a full week at that point is that my surgical assistant requested the time away. I traveled with my daughter and my parents to Jackson Hole, Wyoming, and aside from a few hiccups trying to run payroll remotely, I left work at work. We hiked, rode horses, rafted down the Snake River, and saw eagles and moose. We enjoyed the cool, crisp mountain air, had leisurely lunches, and even took naps. I stepped way out of my comfort zone and went hang gliding, literally learning to "fly."

From that summer on, I have taken at least one full week off every year. These days, I take long weekends off every quarter, with one ten-day to two-week trip at least once a year and a week off with family over the Christmas holidays. That does not include trips that involve continuing education, because as fun and inspiring as those trips can be, they are still work-related. I have been much happier, and frankly more productive when I am in the office, because I can step away from my practice and no longer allow it to be the sole priority of my life. As Dr. Alan Kwong Hing and Christopher Barrow said in their book with Michael Gerber, *The E-Myth Dentist*, "To be more successful, take more holidays."[8]

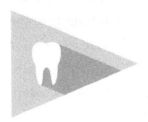

"TO BE MORE SUCCESSFUL, TAKE MORE HOLIDAYS."

—MICHAEL GERBER,
DR. ALAN KWONG HING,
AND CHRISTOPHER BARROW,
THE E-MYTH DENTIST

In addition to taking time out of the office, I fully believe it is possible to create and stick to the daily schedule you want and attract the supporting staff that aligns with your working hours.

When I entered private practice as an associate in 2004, the practice was open Monday through Friday from 7:30 a.m. to 4:00 p.m., except for Wednesday afternoons, when my boss attended his standing men's golf game at the local country club. I negotiated to work a half day on Fridays. At that time, my first husband was the head football coach at a local high school, and I wanted to make sure I could prepare for the Friday night games, including driving to away games. When I purchased the practice two years later, I decided to quit working on Fridays altogether. I knew the team would enjoy the time off, but I also knew they didn't want to take a pay cut. I added Wednesday afternoons back to our working hours and adjusted the team's hourly rates to help offset the difference in hours worked. Soon, we all got to enjoy three-day weekends.

The next big schedule change happened when my daughter began attending kindergarten. By then, I was divorced and trying to navigate the new responsibilities of shared custody and the time constraints of limited before- and after-school programs. I also wanted to be one of the moms waiting in the car pickup line after school. To pull that off, I had to change our schedule to Monday through Thursday, 7:30 a.m. to 3:00 p.m. I was the last one in the door every single morning. Two days a week, I was also the first one out the door so I could secure my place in the car line in time. Even though my daughter is a junior in high school now and can drive herself to and from school, the schedule has remained unchanged for ten-plus years. It is still conducive to the lifestyle my team and I have come to know and appreciate. We have found patients to be far more accommodating of and agreeable to our hours than I ever dreamed. If we lost any patients due to our schedule changes, we haven't noticed.

I have never regretted taking more time away from the practice. When asked by young dentists for advice as they start their careers, I always tell them to make sure they take enough time away from their practice and that if they don't already have a week blocked off for vacation within the next twelve months, they need to block it off the next time they're at the office.

CHECK YOUR SCHEDULE FOR THE NEXT TWELVE MONTHS. MAKE SURE YOU HAVE AT LEAST ONE FULL WEEK BLOCKED OFF FOR A VACATION.

As long as it took for me to feel comfortable taking time away from the office and deciding on a schedule that fit my needs, it took me even longer to realize I also had to dedicate non-patient time to my practice. Around 2015, a handful of business consultants and experts started suggesting that dentists need to make time to work *on* their businesses, not just *in* their practices as dentists. I would roll my eyes and tune this out. For one thing, I didn't know much about the business side of dentistry, and *I didn't have the time for one more thing.* I was still of the mindset that to make more money, I had to produce more, and that meant I had to be the one doing the dentistry. It was the one job I couldn't delegate. I compromised by delegating as many of the non-dental tasks as possible until I learned my lesson with Stacie. Systems and delegation will work, but as owners, we must still be the project managers of any delegated tasks.

As my mom has always told me, "No one cares as much about your business as you do." Hindsight showed me that my mother thought of me as more than a periodontist, professionally. She recognized that I was a business owner, not just the provider within my practice. The point was further hammered home when I read *The E-Myth Dentist.* In the preface, Michael Gerber says, "The key to transforming your practice, and your life, is to grasp the profound difference... between going to work on your practice as an entrepreneur and going to work in your practice as a dentist."[9] When I finally began thinking of my practice as a business and started acting like a DOC, my profitability began to grow.

REASONS YOU MAY NOT CHANGE: NO ONE TAUGHT ME HOW TO RUN A BUSINESS—AND I DON'T WANT TO ANYWAY

"I LIKE DOING DENTISTRY. I don't want to worry about the day-to-day management of my office or team. That's part of why I became a dentist, so I wouldn't have to deal with those things."

I hear this from colleagues over and over. I realize that most of us chose to become dentists to work as clinicians, doing dentistry. I think our lack of confidence in leading teams and managing our businesses relates to the fact that dental schools did not teach us how to run a business; they don't even use the term "business," it's always a "practice." I cannot remember one single class dedicated to understanding financial reports, how to handle insurance reimbursements, collect money from patients, or even how to pay bills. There was no talk of the ebb and flow of collections. I had no idea that I needed to reserve money to help cover the months when there were fewer patients and therefore less production and less money to pay my team and my bills. I never heard the term "Sucktember" to describe the notoriously slow month of September in dental offices until I had been practicing for many years. Most dental practices are true businesses, involving the exchange of a substantial amount of money for the dental services provided. At some point, all dentists must learn something about their numbers, even if that means learning it well after they finish dental school.

In addition to the lack of education on business finances, there was also minimal (if any) discussion at the dental school level about how to find, hire, train, and then retain good employees. We learned the basic roles of the clinical support team members, but none of the other important stuff that related to psychology, team dynamics, and loyalty. Yet, when asked, most dentists will say that dealing with staff is the hardest part of their job. Hardest part.

I am thankful that I worked as an associate before owning a periodontal practice so I could start learning all the things I did not know enough about. As with any other subject I didn't feel adequately prepared for following dental school or my residency, I took courses, listened to webinars, hired consultants, read books or dental publications, asked colleagues, or spoke with experts. While I did not implement everything I learned about, or even understand all the things I now know and plan to review with you in this book, I did learn the basics of collecting money from patients, setting aside enough money to cover months like September, and paying my staff and the other expenses. I hired employees, trained them, and then cross-trained them. I built a loyal team. Up until the moment I was crying into my cheeseburger wrapper, I never had a lack of funds in my business bank account, nor did I suspect that anyone was stealing from me until I found the evidence.

As much as you might prefer to remain completely hands-off in terms of the business—I mean, it's likely you didn't earn an MBA concurrent with your dental degree—to be successful, you will at least have to think like a DOC. Don't worry, you still don't have to be the office manager, approving vacation or ordering supplies; however, you must step away from the operatory every once in a while to oversee your office enough that you don't lose control of your team or business.

REASONS YOU MAY NOT CHANGE: NUMBERS ARE TOO HARD

"I'M JUST NOT GOOD WITH numbers. I was always terrible at math."

When I became a practice owner in 2006, the extent of my knowledge about the "numbers" of my practice was limited to what I learned as an associate. Since I ended up buying the practice I had worked in as an associate, I had a decent idea of the monthly cash flow, including which months might bring in less income than others. Thankfully, there has always been adequate cash in my practice to pay me a salary. Every month, when we collected money from patients and insurance companies, I would pay the bills and initiate the payroll deposits for myself and my team. However, I never knew if I would get any kind of bonus or if my practice had a profit. At the end of the year, I would have to submit the breakdown of outstanding credit card charges as well as any checks that hadn't cleared to my bookkeeper so they could be applied to the appropriate expense accounts. The certified public accountant (CPA) would use that information to do a last-minute tax estimation. This initiated a rush during the last week of the year, when my CPA would have me write a "bonus" check through payroll to deposit into my personal account to "minimize taxes."

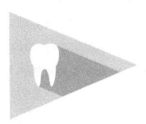 **TAX TIP:** DO NOT FOCUS ALL YOUR ENERGY ON LOWERING YOUR TAXES. INSTEAD, WORK ON INCREASING YOUR PROFIT.

While it was nice to have the extra money in my personal bank account at the end of the year, by the time rent and business loan payments were taken out in early January, my business bank account balance was low enough to make me feel concerned. Somehow, I always managed to produce enough to have the collections needed to cover all my expenses.

If you asked me how much my overhead or operating expenses were, though, or how much of my collections were used to cover my team expenses, I would not have been able to tell you. I also had no idea how much I should be spending on the big expenses in my practice. Nor did I know how many new patients I should be seeing every month to maintain or grow my practice, or what my production needed to be each day to hit my annual goals because, at the time, I wasn't tracking how collections related to production. Thankfully, I did have the historical numbers—what we had done in the past each month in terms of production, collections, procedures, and new patient exams—so I could at least determine patterns.

For many people, *math* is a four-letter word in more ways than one, and they start to zone out when the subject comes up. Don't hate me, but I love math. Yet I still didn't understand my practice numbers. I wasn't sure which key performance indicators (KPIs) mattered or how to use them to track progress. I definitely didn't know how to schedule a day to consistently and predictably reach a certain collection amount, nor was I aware it was something I should try to do.

Unlike algebra, dental numbers can be easily mastered, just like learning how we number teeth, detect cavities, or measure bone loss. Before you finish reading this book, you will know which numbers (or KPIs) matter and how to use them to make sure your business is doing well, predict cash flow, and increase profit. Due to this training, you will also be able to quickly check on whether your practice is on life support or improving as you hike up Profit Mountain.

JUST KEEP CLIMBING

SIT BACK, KEEP READING, AND learn what it takes to have a more successful practice without killing yourself.

GRAB YOUR FAVORITE HIGHLIGHTERS AND A PEN OR PENCIL.

You will want to highlight and write in the margins as you learn how you and your team can enjoy working together to deliver high-quality dental care *and* make more money. It's time to make a commitment that you will no longer rely on having to produce more to make more. No more insanity.

Send me an email at trailblazer@drjuliewoods.com with the subject line "I'm ready to climb" and tell me you will keep reading to learn what it truly takes to have a profitable practice and live the life you want. If you are ready to make this change and either avoid burnout or remember what it was like when you didn't hate dentistry, I want to know. Let's go. Onward to the next flag.

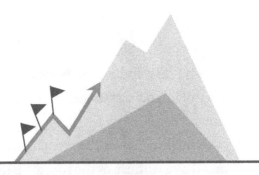

CHAPTER 3
UNDERSTAND
ACCOUNTING BASICS

THE FIRST TIME I HELD a Profit Over Production workshop, I showed up with a box of highlighters, calculators, and worksheets. I was excited! One of my best friends from dental school was in attendance, as well as several other colleagues I had come to know and love over the years. Everyone was jazzed to spend the day with friends, learning to be more profitable. The energy was up. Well, until I had them pull out the first set of financials we would work through together, that is. There wasn't enough coffee in the room to keep those frowns from forming. While one of the hosts made a coffee run, I pressed on.

I knew that this portion of the program would be the longest and most frustrating, and had planned accordingly. I would proceed slowly and encourage participants when they were confused; I had done test runs with my husband acting as a stand-in for someone who didn't understand business financial statements. I purposely used fake financials so that everyone could work together. And I had simplified everything as much as possible because understanding the basics of accounting, or at least the basics of financial statements, was critical to the participants' success.

Still, when it was time to look at the financials, anxiety and panic seem to spread like wildfire in the room. I had forgotten how daunting the tasks I was asking them to complete were. I thought since we were looking at fake numbers, no one would get nervous about the state of their own practice. I was wrong. The fear of not understanding something embarrassed my high-achieving colleagues. I called on one of my friends. "Pennie, you doing okay?" Her response was, "Yeah, but I used to be a wreck before I started working with my new accounting firm. I would drink a glass of wine before every meeting to discuss my practice numbers. I really hate looking at numbers … no offense." It sounded eerily like when patients tell us, "I hate going to the dentist. I don't mean it personally, but I really hate it."

The attendees took deep breaths, worked together, asked pertinent questions, and felt prepared after getting over their initial insecurities and anxiety. The success of that workshop led to numerous others. Many attendees have shared with me that reviewing financial statements with me as their guide, highlighting and explaining things to note in simplified terms, made them feel less anxious and more confident talking about money. They were reassured to know that others in the room felt as intimidated as they did. Some participants told me that the task of highlighting numbers on the fake statements felt very elementary at the time, but they did it anyway. Many have told me that going through the financials together and finding the important figures from the fake statements is what gave them the know-how and confidence to go home and look at their own financials. Using the numbers we found together, they were able to do the calculations presented in the next chapters. They knew my offer to "check their work" was not a hollow one, so they didn't go home and give up like they had when they tried to implement a cash management system like Profit First on their own.

While I know that reading this in a book might not be as entertaining as attending a live workshop, I will still be right here with you as your trail angel, ready to encourage you along the way and point out the things that surprised and stumped those first attendees. Even if your eyes are glazed over by the end of this chapter, you will be better equipped for your climb up Profit Mountain if you understand some basic terminology and how to evaluate your financials. You'll also know the right questions to ask your accounting professionals, which will help you decide whether that team is providing the level of service you need at each stage of your career.

Even though many of your patients aren't big fans of going to the dentist, they do it anyway because they know you have their best interests in mind and are helping them keep their mouths healthy. You might "hate looking at numbers" as much as they hate coming into your office. I would like to reassure you that I have your best interests in mind and am merely trying to assist in your efforts to keep your practice healthy and profitable. I will remind you every so often to stop, rest, and catch your breath. This journey we are on to get you to the top of Profit Mountain is *not* a race. Slow and steady is how we will proceed for now.

TAKE ACTION—GATHER DOCUMENTS

BEFORE READING THE NEXT SECTION of this chapter, go to Appendices 1–3 and make copies of the "Profit Over Production (POP), LLC, Balance Sheet and P&L Before Cash Management," the "Profit Over Production (POP), LLC, Balance Sheet and P&L After Cash Management," and the "Important Numbers Worksheet." If you prefer to download copies of these documents, you can do so at drjuliewoods.com. We are going to work through these two sets of financials together so you will be prepared to find the information in your own documents.

FINANCIAL STATEMENT BASICS

A **BALANCE SHEET** IS A statement of the assets, liabilities, and capital of a business at a particular point in time.

Your balance sheet is broken into two main categories: "Assets" and "Liabilities and Equity." There are many important things to note within each category, and I will briefly go over the line items I want you to find and highlight.

1. **Cash on Hand** – At the very top of your balance sheet is a section labeled "Assets." You will be able to find the total amount of money in your bank accounts within that category. You may only have one checking account for all your business needs, or perhaps one account for direct deposits from insurance, one account for all the money received in your office via checks, credit cards, and cash,

and maybe a savings account. Before I implemented Profit First, I had one account to handle all my business needs. Now, I have *nine* accounts. That's right, nine! The joke amongst Profit First Professionals is, "When in doubt, create an account." In layman's terms, that merely means if there is something you specifically want to track or budget for, you create an account for that expense and limit your spending to the percentage you set for that expenditure. For now, I just want you to find and highlight the total of "cash" listed for POP, LLC, before cash management and write it in the Important Numbers Worksheet.

When we did this at the workshop, I showed an example of a balance sheet with a negative bank account balance. When no one seemed to question it, I quickly pointed it out to them and asked if their banks minded when their accounts dipped below a zero balance. A hand shot up and someone asked, "So how is that even possible? Is the account really below zero?" I let them know it was one of my first indicators that this dentist was in financial trouble, but also it was likely the balance was not currently below zero and the "books" were just not up-to-date. To double-check the accuracy of your bookkeeping and specifically if everything is reconciled, look at the balance sheet that ends on the date of the most recent last quarter and compare the cash on hand numbers to the bank statements for the same month. Any account balance listed should match (to the penny) what is reported on the same month's bank statement.

BALANCE SHEET Before Cash Management		
ASSETS	**TOTAL**	
Current Assets		
Bank Accounts		46,792.00
Total Bank Accounts	**$**	**46,792.00**
Fixed Assets		
Leasehold Improvements		258,385.52
Furniture		126,417.60
Equipment		118,440.88
Accumulated Depreciation		−502,056.00
Total Fixed Assets	**$**	**1,188.00**
Other Assets		
Goodwill		475,977.39
Loan Closing Costs		709.61
Accumulated Amortization		−333,479.00
Total Other Assets	**$**	**143,208.00**
TOTAL ASSETS	**$**	**191,188.00**

Figure 3.1: Assets Section of POP, LLC,
Before Cash Management Balance Sheet

If the cash on hand total listed on your balance sheet is a negative number, that should be your first hint that your bookkeeping is not up-to-date. Most banks will not allow you to carry a negative account balance.

2. **Long-Term Debt** – Under the "Liabilities" section, you will find both current and long-term debt. Current debt might list upcoming payroll, or your credit card balance. What I want you to find and record is the total of your *long-term debt*, as it is one of your overhead expenses that doesn't show up on your profit and loss (P&L) statement as a current expenditure. Some financials will report the "Current Portion of Long-Term Debt," but what I want you to find, highlight and record on your worksheet is the *total long-term debt*.

3. **Distributions** – Moving down the balance sheet to the "Equity" section, you will see line item(s) for shareholder draws/distributions. *Please note that Before Cash Management, no shareholder distributions are listed as none were taken. Sometimes, these are further divided into tax distributions, personal distributions, or distributions for student loan debt. This is the place where any non-payroll wages are reported. Highlight the total shareholder distributions and record that number on your worksheet.

BALANCE SHEET Before Cash Management	
LIABILITIES AND EQUITY	**TOTAL**
Long-Term Liabilities	
Note Payable – Practice Purchase	113,871.72
Note Payable – Computer Hardware	23,941.25
Note Payable – Leasehold Improvements	124,870.03
Total Long-Term Liabilities	$ **262,683.00**

Equity		
Capital Stock		1,000
Retained Earnings		−143,078.00
Net Income		−3,096.00
Total Equity	$	**(145,174.00)**
TOTAL LIABILITIES AND EQUITY	$	**191,188.00**

**Figure 3.2: Long-Term Liabilities and Distributions
of POP, LLC, Before Cash Management Balance Sheet**

Below, you will see what the balance sheet portion of your Important Numbers Worksheet should look like for POP, LLC, before cash management.

BALANCE SHEET-RELATED

Cash on Hand $46,792

Long-Term Debt $262,683

Distributions   0

Tax Basis/Equity ($145,174)

**Figure 3.3: Balance Sheet Portion of Important Numbers
Worksheet for POP, LLC, Before Cash Management**

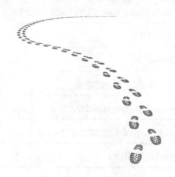

Before we move on to evaluating the profit and loss statement, I want you to take a mental and physical break. I know this exercise can be daunting, not only because it is not a clinical procedure you have done over and over again, but also because you are likely beginning to worry about the information your financial statements might reveal. I have been in your shoes. I know how scary this can feel and how much anxiety it can produce. When I first went through this process, I also felt angry that I had "let this happen" to my practice. So—breathe. Remember, I am living proof that it's never too late to start the journey to the top of Profit Mountain so you can master cash management and practice the way you want!

The **profit and loss (P&L) statement, aka income statement**, is a listing of the chart of accounts that shows the amount of money the practice has collected, how much it has spent, and the total profit (or loss) it has made during a particular period.

When I purchased my practice back in 2004, I continued using the accounting firm that the previous periodontist had used. I did that for continuity and simplicity, as I barely remembered high school accounting, much less how to read financial reports. My chart of accounts was set up in alphabetical order, as it had been previously. I purposely set up the POP, LLC, "before" financials in a similar fashion. While I was able to find the information I needed, once I switched my books to a more user-friendly chart of accounts that was set up according to dental industry standards (where like expenses are grouped), it was even easier to see the percentage of my total collections that I spent on each category. For example, rather than having to search for health insurance, retirement contributions, team wages, team payroll taxes, and uniforms on the alphabetical listing and then calculate the total percentage of collections spent on team expenses, I could now readily ascertain that information because it was all grouped. The "after" profit and loss statement for POP, LLC, (see Figure 3.15, pp.67-70) will give you an idea of how my chart of accounts is currently set up.

When you use this chapter as a reference to find and highlight items in your own profit and loss statements, you will quickly find out how organized your chart of accounts is and can make changes as necessary. You may use the fake financial statements provided as an example for your existing accountant and ask them to create something similar using your data. As we go through this together, I will show and explain the differences you might come across when looking at your own numbers. For now, have your highlighter handy and let's work through the important line items to note and record from the "before" profit and loss statement for POP, LLC:

1. **Total Income** – This is what we refer to as our "collections." Ideally, this number will include all the money that was deposited into the practice from patients and insurance companies, minus any refunds given. I also prefer to subtract the credit card fees here since that portion of

the patient's payment never actually makes it into the business bank account. Depending on how your chart of accounts is set up, that particular line item might be listed later as a credit card or merchant services processing fee.

PROFIT AND LOSS STATEMENT Before Cash Management	
	TOTAL
Income	
Fee Income	963,051
Refunds	−16,690
Total Income	$ **946,361**

Figure 3.4: Total Income for POP, LLC,
Before Cash Management Profit and Loss Statement

2. **Net Income** – The number we commonly refer to as our profit (or loss). It will be listed at the very end of your profit and loss statement.

3. **Owner's Compensation** – As I mentioned before, this amount is sometimes mixed in with the other payroll numbers. You need to record not only the owner's payroll wages, but also the owner's portion of the payroll taxes, the cost of their health insurance, and any other benefits the owner receives due to being the owner, such as having their children on the payroll. Based on what

you can ascertain on this "before" statement, the owner does not have children on the payroll, nor are they paying for their own health insurance. You can record the total of all these elements on your worksheet. Do *not* include any shareholder distributions that might have been taken. You already found and recorded that aspect of owner's compensation when we reviewed the balance sheet. The payroll taxes highlighted on the "before" profit and loss statement include both the owner's and the team's payroll taxes. Therefore, you will need to figure out what portion of the taxes are actually associated with the owner. You can get the most accurate number by pulling payroll reports. Or, to guesstimate, you can use the following formula:

$$\frac{\text{Salary} - \text{Dr.} \times \text{Taxes} - \text{Payroll}}{\text{Salary} - \text{Dr.} + \text{Salary} - \text{Staff}} = \text{Owner's Portion of Payroll Taxes}$$

$$\frac{\$258,000 \times \$31,012}{\$520,922} = \$15,360$$

Figure 3.5: Formula to Guesstimate the Owner's Portion of Payroll Taxes

PROFIT AND LOSS STATEMENT Before Cash Management		
		TOTAL
Expenses		
Salaries – Staff		262,922
Salary – Doctor		258,000
Taxes – Payroll		31,012
Telephone		8,189
Training and Education		2,111
Travel and Conventions		11,561
Uniforms		2,142
Utilities		1,565
Total Expenses	$	**949,457**
NET INCOME	$	**(3,096)**

Figure 3.6: Owner's Salary and Net Income for POP, LLC,
Before Cash Management Profit and Loss Statement

4. **Interest Expense** – On the "before" chart of accounts, this value can be found in the alphabetical listing; however, on the "after" chart of accounts, it is located at the very bottom of the report, just above "Net Income." This expense is the portion of your long-term debt that can be used to lower your tax burden during the year and includes any interest you have paid on your current liabilities, such as credit cards.

PROFIT AND LOSS STATEMENT Before Cash Management	
	TOTAL
Expenses	
Accounting and Data Processing	67,288
Amortization Expense	31,828
Bank Charges	11,662
Business Promotion	10,646
Contract Labor	3,194
Contributions	3,450
Depreciation	7,304
Dues – Non-Deductable	200
Dues – Professional	4,503
Insurance – Operating	8,504
Interest Expense	18,022

Figure 3.7: Interest Expense, Depreciation, and Amortization from the POP, LLC, Before Cash Management Profit and Loss Statement

5. **Taxes** – This number will be relatively low and is related to any property tax, sales tax, or "use tax" the business has paid during the time frame evaluated. This is *not* where payroll taxes are recorded.

6. **Depreciation** – This expense is related to the reduction in the value of an *asset* (a dental chair, for example) over time due to wear and tear. This is one of two expenses that does not involve a cash expenditure on your part.

7. **Amortization** – This expense is related to a reduction in the value of an *intangible asset* (for example, goodwill) over some time. It is the second expense that does not relate to actual cash leaving your practice. This will be considered when you conduct your Limited Financial Exam.

▶ **PROFIT AND LOSS STATEMENT-RELATED**

Total Income $946,361

Net Income   ($3,096)

Owner's Compensation

    Owner's Salary $258,000

    Owner's Payroll Taxes $15,360

    Children's Salaries   None

    Children's Payroll Taxes   None

    Health Insurance   None

    Total = $273,360

Interest Expense $18,022

Taxes   None

Depreciation $7,304

Amortization $31,828

EBITDA

Figure 3.8: POP, LLC, Before Cash Management Portion
of the Important Numbers Worksheet

You might have noticed that several of the numbers recorded on your worksheet are bracketed. These are the numbers that will be used to calculate your EBITDA. EBITDA is the acronym for "earnings before interest, taxes, depreciation, or amortization." EBITDA is a measure of a company's overall financial performance or profitability and is used as an alternative to net income in some instances. It has become more widely known within dental circles with the influx of private equity and dental service organizations (DSOs). In dentistry, the range of a healthy EBITDA value is 30-50% of collections, and examples of how to calculate EBITDA value will be presented later in this chapter.

EBITDA Calculation
(Goal is 30-50%)

Net Income

Owner Compensation

Interest Expense

Taxes

Depreciation

\+   Amortization

\=   EBITDA Value

$$\frac{\text{EBITDA Value} \times 100}{\text{Total Income}} = \text{EBITDA Percentage of Collections}$$

Figure 3.9: EBITDA Formula

EBITDA Calculation for POP, LLC
Before Cash Management

$$-\$3,096 \quad \text{Net Income}$$
$$\$273,360 \quad \text{Owner's Compensation}$$
$$\$18,022 \quad \text{Interest Expense}$$
$$\$0 \quad \text{Taxes}$$
$$\$7,304 \quad \text{Depreciation}$$
$$+ \quad \$31,828 \quad \text{Amortization}$$
$$= \quad \$327,418 \quad \text{EBITDA value}$$

$$\frac{\$327,418}{\$946,361} \times 100\% = 35\%$$

Figure 3.10: EBITDA Calculation for POP, LLC, Before Cash Management

8. **Team Expenses** – The total of *all* the expenses related to your team. This includes their wages, payroll taxes, health insurance, retirement contributions, the cost of maintaining the retirement plan, uniforms, and any expenditures for their continuing education or travel. Team expenses are confined to the supporting members of the staff that aid in delivering clinical care and running the business. It should *not* include any of the expenses related to the owner or any associates working in the practice. Those numbers should be separated out and not used when comparing your team expenses to dental industry standards. If you have temporary staff, or if you have been

paying for services to be done offsite that are traditionally handled by a nonclinical team member, you also need to include that amount when calculating team expenses. Examples include paying for insurance verifications or billing services.

9. **Facilities** – This item includes rent, repairs, and maintenance on your office and utilities.

10. **Dental Supplies** – These are all the professional supplies used daily to complete patient care. In my periodontal practice, that includes bone-grafting materials, collagen membranes, and implants. I subdivide those surgical supply expenses so I can quickly see if a certain supply expense stays roughly the same from month to month. If not, I make sure that the increase in supplies correlates to an increase in osseous regenerative or implant placement procedures.

11. **Lab Expenses** – This includes all fees paid to outside labs, both restorative and relating to clear aligners or other orthodontic appliances. If you do in-house restorations such as CEREC, you should include your material costs in this expense.

12. **Marketing** – This item encompasses all business promotions done for your practice. This is where I record any expenses related to my website, giveaways to patients, gifts

to referring offices, and advertisements on the internet and in print media.

13. **Office Supplies/Expenses** – This should be a relatively small expense compared to some of the others, but since it was the expense that alerted me to theft within my practice, I always evaluate it when reviewing others' financials. Office supplies and expenses include things like copy paper, printer cartridges, toilet paper, etc.

PROFIT AND LOSS STATEMENT Before Cash Management	
	TOTAL
Expenses	
Bank Charges	11,662
Business Promotion	10,646
Contract Labor	3,194
Contributions	3,450
Depreciation	7,304
Dues – Non-Deductible	200
Dues – Professional	4,503
Insurance – Operating	8,504
Interest Expense	18,022
Lab Costs	2,719
Legal and Professional	4,291
Meals and Entertainment	1,775
Meetings – Professional	750
Miscellaneous	332

PROFIT AND LOSS STATEMENT Before Cash Management	
	TOTAL
Expenses	
Office Supplies and Expenses	32,497
Professional Supplies	108,053
Rent	33,600
Repairs and Maintenance	495
Retirement Plan Expense	3,576
Safe Harbor Contribution	17,266
Salaries – Staff	262,922
Salary – Doctor	258,000
Taxes – Payroll	31,012
Telephone	8,189
Training and Education	2,111
Travel and Conventions	11,561
Uniforms	2,142
Utilities	1,565

Figure 3.11: Highlighted Expenses from the POP, LLC,
Before Cash Management Profit and Loss Statement

14. **Associate Pay** – If you don't employ any associates, you will record a zero on your worksheet. Those of you with multiple associates and benefits should record the total amount on the worksheet.

Next is what the other portion of the Important Numbers Worksheet should look like for POP, LLC, Before Cash Management.

▷ PROFIT AND LOSS STATEMENT-RELATED

Team Expenses

Staff Payroll _____ $262,922

Contract Labor _____ $3,194

Staff Insurance _____ None

Retirement _____ $3,576 + $17,266

Staff Payroll Taxes _____ $15,652

Payroll Processing ___ Not separated out

Uniforms and Laundry _____ $2,142

Staff Recruitment ___ Not separated out

Total Team Expenses = _____ $304,752

Facilities

Rent _____ $33,600

Repairs and Maintenance _____ $495

Utilities _____ $1,565

Total Facilities = _____ $35,660

Dental Supplies $108,053

Lab Expenses $2,719

Marketing $10,646

Office Supplies and Expense $32,497

Associate Compensation

Salary _____

Payroll Taxes _____

Health Insurance _____

Other Benefits _____

Total Associate Compensation = ___ None

**Figure 3.12: POP, LLC, Before Cash Management Portion
of the Important Numbers Worksheet**

"AFTER CASH MANAGEMENT" FINANCIAL STATEMENT ANALYSIS

TIME FOR ANOTHER BREAK. STAND up, get some caffeine, or take a walk outside. Come back when you're ready to see what the "after" financials reveal. I have included this information so you have another example to use as a reference before you begin looking for the numbers within your own documents. First, we will see what changes are evident after cash management by looking at "Total Bank Accounts," "Total Long-Term Liabilities," and "Distributions" from the "after" balance sheet.

BALANCE SHEET After Cash Management	
ASSETS	**TOTAL**
Current Assets	
Bank Accounts	
Income	5,000.00
Profit	2,211.86
Owner's Compensation	4,423.72
Overhead	12,165.23
Tax Reserves	3,317.79
Vault	130,000.00
Total Bank Accounts	$ 157,118.60
Fixed Assets	
Leasehold Improvements	258,385.52
Furniture	126,417.60
Equipment	157,960.81
Accumulated Depreciation	−542,763.93
Total Fixed Assets	$ 0.00

Other Assets		
Goodwill		475,000.00
Loan Closing Costs		1,687.00
Accumulated Amortization		−476,687.00
Security Deposits		3,018.49
Total Other Assets	$	**3,018.49**
TOTAL ASSETS	$	**160,137.09**
LIABILITIES AND EQUITY		**TOTAL**
Liabilities		
Current Liabilities		
Credit Card		13,584.82
Payroll Liabilities		0.00
Accrued 401(K)		30,758.09
Total Current Liabilities	$	**44,342.91**
Long-Term Liabilities		
Note Payable – Practice Purchase		0.00
Note Payable – Computer Hardware		0.00
Note Payable – Leasehold Improvements		0.00
PPP Loan #1		0.00
PPP Loan #2		0.00
Total Long-Term Liabilities	$	**–**
Equity		
Capital Stock		1,000
Retained Earnings		79,700.46
Distributions		
Personal		−1,372.49
Taxes		−83,435.97
Net Income		208,588.00
Total Equity	$	**$ 204,480.00**
TOTAL LIABILITIES AND EQUITY	$	**160,137.09**

Figure 3.13: POP, LLC, After Cash Management Balance Sheet

Cash on hand, which is equivalent to the total of all the bank accounts, is now over $157,000, whereas before it was under $47,000. In Chapter 9, I will discuss how to calculate the amount of cash you would like to have on hand to equal a minimum of ninety calendar days' expenses. For now, trust that this dentist currently has roughly seventy-five days' worth of expenses covered (as opposed to less than twenty days' worth before cash management). I will use both financials to show you how to calculate the BAM—or "bare-ass minimum"—needed.

BALANCE SHEET-RELATED

Cash on Hand	$157,119
Long-Term Debt	None
Distributions	$85,808
Tax Basis/Equity	$204,480

Figure 3.14: Balance Sheet Portion of Important Numbers Worksheet for POP, LLC, After Cash Management

Other exciting information we can glean by looking at this financial statement includes the fact that this dentist is now 100% debt-free, with no more long-term debts owed. Additionally, this DOC has been using distributions to cover their quarterly estimated tax payments, as noted in the "Distributions" section.

In the following chapters, I will show you *how* implementing a cash management system allowed this dentist to make steady progress on their climb to the summit of Profit Mountain, but you can see some of the obvious changes merely by evaluating the "after" profit and loss statement. Most significant is that the staff cost was virtually unchanged, while collections went up by about $40,000. Surprisingly, the dental supply costs actually decreased. This is most likely due to the use of both better systems for ordering and more than one vendor. The fluctuation in office supplies/expenses and marketing costs has more to do with accurate bookkeeping than any actual changes for this particular dentist. If you are worried about the decline in owner's compensation, remember that the net income is now over $200,000, while previously it was just below zero. That means the overall profitability is indeed UP! I will review the specifics in the next few chapters when I explain the dental industry standards for various expenses.

PROFIT AND LOSS STATEMENT After Cash Management		
		TOTAL
Income		
Fee Income		1,006,900
Refunds		−8,601
Merchant Fees		−11,372
Total Income	$	**986,927**
Expenses		
Team Expenses		
Assistant Wages		42,038

Administrative Wages		74,360
Hygiene Wages		127,214
Contract Labor Wages		1,652
Staff Insurance Benefits		12,439
Staff Retirement Plan		3,488
Payroll Taxes		18,610
Payroll Processing Fees		4,662
Uniforms and Laundry		4,819
Staff Recruitment		2,425
Total Team Expenses	$	**291,707**
Advertising and Marketing		
Advertising and Promotion		26,548
Total Marketing Expenses	$	**26,548**
Dental Supplies		
Dental Supplies		84,523
Hazardous Waste Disposal Fees		2,549
Total Dental Supplies	$	**87,072**
Lab Expenses		
Lab Fees		3,304
Total Lab Expenses	$	**3,304**
Rent and Facilities		
Rent		43,200
Utilities		2,461
Facility Repairs and Maintenance		1,065
Janitorial Expense		200
Security		906
Total Rent and Facilities	$	**47,832**
Equipment and Furniture		

Small Equipment and Furniture		744
Equipment Repairs and Maintenance		921
Computer Support and Maintenance		14,482
Total Equipment and Furniture	$	**16,147**
General and Administrative		
Legal		2,642
Collections		2,096
Accounting		16,700
Consulting		29,724
Insurance–Business		6,789
Licenses and Permits		1,661
Dues, Journals, and Subscriptions		968
State PTE Tax		1,000
Bank Service Charges		98
Continuing Education		1,109
Conventions and Seminars		2,988
Travel Expense		6,432
Automobile Expense		102
Meals		2,892
Office Supplies and Expenses		11,725
Postage		4,210
Telephone		10,403
Total General and Admin	$	**101,539**
Total Expenses	$	**574,149**
NET OPERATING INCOME	$	**412,778**
Other Income		
Interest Income		114
Total Other Income	$	**114**

Other Expenses		
Owner Doctor Compensation		
Doctor Wages		150,000
Doctor Payroll Taxes		11,784
Doctor Health Insurance		13,217
Doctor Family Wages		12,210
Doctor Family Payroll Taxes		1,099
Total Owner Doctor Compensation	$	**188,310**
Amortization		0
Depreciation		15,994
Interest Expense		0
Total Other Expenses	$	**204,304**
NET OTHER INCOME	$	**(204,190)**
NET INCOME	$	**208,588**

Figure 3.15: After Cash Management Profit and Loss
Statement for POP, LLC

POSITIVE CHANGES TO EBITDA

THE CALCULATION TO ARRIVE AT the dollar EBITDA value
involves taking your reported net income and adding owner's
compensation, taxes, interest expense, depreciation, and
amortization as listed on your profit and loss statements. The
higher the dollar amount, the better. Again, as a percentage of
collections, the EBITDA goal is 30–50%. This metric is often
used in the business world to express the value of a business for
potential purchasers. In the dental world, it's being used more
and more as DSOs and private equity firms purchase practices.

——————— EBITDA ———————

Earnings Before Interest Expense, Taxes, Depreciation, and Amortization

How non-dental businesses
evaluate the value of something.

Often, DSOs and private equity firms
offer a purchase price of between 5-9 times
your EBIDTA value, which is how you could
potentially sell your practice for more than
100% of your average collections.

Target: 30-50% of collections

**Figure 3.16: How You Could Potentially Get More than 100%
of Collections with the Sale of Your Business**

This dentist has not only increased the whole dollar amount of their earnings, but also increased the EBITDA percentage of collections value by 7%. While both periods evaluated show a value within the goal range of 30–50%, 42% of collections would definitely be more appealing to a potential buyer—and certainly to any commercial lender.

EBITDA Calculation for POP, LLC
Before Cash Management

	$	−3,096	Net Income
	$	273,360	Owner Compensation
	$	18,022	Interest Expense
	$	0	Taxes
	$	7,304	Depreciation
+	$	31,828	Amortization
	$	327,418	EBITDA Value

EBITDA as a percentage of income:

$$\frac{\$327,418}{\$946,361} \times 100\% = 35\%$$

EBITDA Calculation for POP, LLC
After Cash Management

	$	208,588	Net Income
	$	188,310	Owner Compensation
	$	0	Interest Expense
	$	1,000	Taxes
	$	15,994	Depreciation
+	$	0	Amortization
	$	413,892	EBITDA Value

EBITDA as a percentage of income:

$$\frac{\$413,892}{\$986,927} \times 100\% = 42\%$$

Figure 3.17: EBITDA Comparisons of "Before" and "After" Cash Management

BREAK TIME

WHAT WE HAVE DONE SO far is much like reviewing a patient's medical history. I know how daunting it may seem to look for these values on fake financials, so I know it's a big deal when you prepare to "face" your own numbers. I want to remind you that when you look at accounting statements, you review what has *previously* happened within your dental practice. Accounting statements only show what has already transpired and been recorded. That is one of the limitations of trying to use financial reports to help you navigate for the future.

By continuing to read this book and do the exercises, *you can change the FUTURE of your practice!* So, rest a minute and celebrate all the hard work you just did. If you are like me, it will take some time for these new terms to "marinate" in your head before you begin to understand them.

If you haven't yet pulled your own financial statements and printed out the Important Numbers Worksheet, do so now. After you take some time to regroup, highlight the important values and record the numbers so you will be prepared for the next chapters.

THINGS TO CONSIDER WHEN EVALUATING YOUR PROFESSIONAL TEAM

YOUR NEEDS WILL NATURALLY CHANGE as you progress through the various stages of practice ownership. As a new practice owner, whether you purchase an existing practice or start your own, I think it would be helpful to have your chart of accounts set up to the dental industry standards. Figure 3.15 shows an example chart of accounts, which can also be downloaded at drjuliewoods.com.

You can certainly utilize this chapter to help you get familiar with where important numbers are located on your financial reports. In later chapters, you will discover more of the "secrets" your financial reports and patient software can reveal. The sustainability of your practice is paramount to your health, financial and otherwise. The hardest step on the journey of ownership is already behind you. Now it's all about continuing to put one foot in front of the other. With the basics you learned in this chapter, you are ready to take a closer look at your numbers and figure out just where you are on the climb up the mountain.

CHAPTER 4
DETERMINE IF YOU'RE PROFITABLE ENOUGH

I OWNED MY PRACTICE FOR over a dozen years before I started to learn about the difference between profit and salary. Up until that point, I decided somewhat arbitrarily how much to pay myself each month. Then, at the end of the year, I did as my CPA told me and rushed to get my "bonus" check cashed in time. I usually had extra money in the business bank account, but I didn't understand the best way to grow that money besides letting it sit in my main checking account or a savings account earning negligible interest. Why hadn't anyone suggested that I use the benefits of profit sharing to put more money away in my 401(k), or in a defined benefit plan? I only learned about those options from seeing other business owners' posts in online dental groups.

"Do I make enough money to add profit sharing to my 401(k) and stash even more money in my retirement accounts?" I asked my financial planner. "Wouldn't that also help lower my taxes?"

After reviewing my financials again, they finally took me seriously and helped me switch over to a new pension company that made the necessary changes so I could begin maximizing that option the very next calendar year. Conversations then ensued with the new pension company owner. We discussed how I wanted my "salary" to be significantly higher than those of the rest of my team to keep the costs of the profit sharing lower.

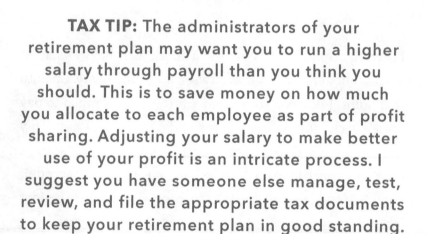

TAX TIP: The administrators of your retirement plan may want you to run a higher salary through payroll than you think you should. This is to save money on how much you allocate to each employee as part of profit sharing. Adjusting your salary to make better use of your profit is an intricate process. I suggest you have someone else manage, test, review, and file the appropriate tax documents to keep your retirement plan in good standing.

SALARY VERSUS PROFIT

I HAD BEEN PRACTICING FOR over ten years before the pension company owner finally helped me understand the difference between salary and profit distributions. The *Merriam-Webster Dictionary* defines "salary" as "fixed compensation paid regularly for services."[10] In *Simple Numbers, Straight Talk, Big Profits!*, Greg Crabtree writes, "You get paid a salary for what you do."[11] Therefore, you need to figure out a market-based wage for the dentistry you provide in your community.

The easiest way to figure out your salary range and median is to look up the "dentist salary" link at drjuliewoods.com. While there is some variation across the country, $150,000 is a good rule of thumb for a dentist's annual salary. Experts agree that you must learn to live off your salary. Therefore, the money you pay yourself as a salary is the *only* money from the practice that you should consider when budgeting for your personal living expenses. If you live in a state that does not allow for an S corporation designation, then you might not run any of your salary through payroll. If that is the case, you will take money out of the practice as distributions. Even if you pay yourself solely through distributions, you need to pay yourself what you would pay a dentist to fill in for you.

If you cannot afford to pay yourself a market-based wage, then you are not profitable enough. It's important to realize that if you are consistently underpaying yourself, your business is sick.

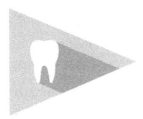

PAYING YOURSELF A LOWER SALARY TO SAVE MONEY ON PAYROLL TAXES CAN TRIGGER AN IRS TAX AUDIT.

The *Merriam-Webster Dictionary* defines "profit" as "the excess of returns over expenditure in a series of transactions" or the "net income usually for a given period of time."[12] In *Profit First,* Mike Michalowicz turns those definitions upside down by having you take profit out *before* spending on other expenses. His definition is, "Profit is simple: cash in the bank. Cold. Hard. Cash."[13]

Most of us know we should be paid something for doing all this dentistry but, as I mentioned earlier, we may be unsure if we are making enough money to be considered profitable. How much is enough?

BREAKING EVEN IS NOT ENOUGH

ALL BUSINESSES, INCLUDING YOUR DENTAL practice, should aim to be profitable. A study done by Jessie Hagen of U.S. Bank found that a poor understanding of cash flow contributes to the failure of small businesses 82% of the time.[14] In other words, "a lack of profitability is consistently the major reason cited for business discontinuation."[15] We know this instinctively. If we are merely breaking even on normal expenses, all it takes is one broken air compressor or weather-related closure before we are in crisis mode.

There is a whole chapter in *Simple Numbers, Straight Talk, Big Profits!* dedicated to profit titled "Profit: Why 10 Percent Is the New Breakeven." The author compares businesses that earn 5% or less of pretax profit to people on life support.[16] Much like if your heart stopped beating, if you stop making a profit in your practice, your business rapidly declines. Thankfully, we have the equivalent of an automated external defibrillator (AED) to jump-start your practice back into profitability.

To quickly figure out your pretax profit for the previous year, pull up the profit and loss statement for that year, or locate the Important Numbers Worksheet you filled out in the last chapter and find two key numbers. First, locate the number recorded as "Total Income," which is equivalent to the number of collections you received. Now, find the value for "Net Income." Use those two numbers to calculate your pretax profit using the following formula:

$$\frac{\text{Net Income}}{\text{Total Income}} \times 100 = \text{Pretax Profit}$$

Figure 4.1: Pretax Profit Formula

According to Crabtree, your business is profitable *enough* if your pretax profit is a minimum of 10%.[17] However, if your debt payments equal 10% or more of your collections, you may still not be "profitable enough." I will explain a bit more about exactly what I mean by this in the next section. If you are taking home a market-based salary and your pretax profit is more than 15%, then you can rest assured your business is *great*, at least from a cash management standpoint.

As long as the owner dentist is being paid a reasonable salary of $120,000–$180,000, a quick measure of financial stability is to divide net income by total income and multiply by 100%.

5% or less means your business is on life support

10% means your business is at the breakeven point

15% or more means your business is doing great

Source: Greg Crabtree[18]

Using the information you recorded on the Important Numbers Worksheet for POP, LLC, let's evaluate the pretax profit for "before" and "after." Right off the bat, you should see that the "before" net income was a negative number, so the practice was in trouble for sure. After implementing cash management, the dentist's pretax profit is now 21%, which means the practice has not only avoided "death" but is doing well!

"BEFORE"   "AFTER"

$$\frac{-\$3,096}{\$946,361} \times 100\% = 0.3\%$$

$$\frac{\$208,588}{\$986,361} \times 100\% = 21\%$$

Figure 4.2: Pretax Profit Calculations for POP, LLC

SHOW ME THE MONEY

FOR THE FIRST DOZEN YEARS of my practice, I couldn't find my profit. My profit and loss statement showed that I had a profit, but I would say to myself, *Why doesn't my net income match my bank account balance?* I looked at my P&L and wanted to scream—like Jerry Maguire—*"Show me the money!"*[19] I did not understand that only the interest expense was recorded on my P&L when I paid money toward my business loan every month. I certainly did not understand that there were non-cash expenses, such as depreciation and amortization, recorded on the P&L that affected the number recorded as "profit" or "loss."

It was only after I read *Profit First* that the reason my bank account balance did not match the number reported on the P&L finally started to click. In the book, Mike outlines detailed instructions on how to perform an "Instant Assessment" to evaluate the finances of your business.[20] I am about to explain how to do a Limited Financial Exam. I think that sounds better than "Instant Assessment for Dental Dummies." Also, this method is more streamlined and appropriate to our industry.

If you are thinking, *I know I have a problem, I just need to know how to fix it,* the Limited Financial Exam is what you need for a proper diagnosis so you can work on any problems detected. If your exam shows no significant problems at this time, then no big changes need to be made. As is true for our patients' health, the health of your practice is dependent on what you do, regularly, to make it better or at least maintain it. Regular checkups will help keep you on track. Maybe it is my bias as a periodontist, but I think you need to conduct Limited Financial Exams quarterly. This will involve more than just receiving the quarterly reports from your accountant. You will need to access the financial wellness of your business by doing this limited evaluation. If you don't want to be the one responsible for performing the exam, a Profit First Professional like me can certainly be used as your diagnostician.

LIMITED FINANCIAL EXAM

To perform your Limited Financial Exam (LFE), you will need to gather a few things. These tools are like your perio probe, dental explorer, and set of radiographs. If you have access to your accounting software and the internet, this is a toothbrushing-length exercise. If you must wait for your accountant to get you some of the info, it may take a little longer. Once you have the documents, it will take you less than the time of a crown preparation to work through the exercise.

If you don't have immediate access to your financial statements, you can work through the information you gathered using the financial statements for POP, LLC. To perform an

LFE, you will need the Limited Financial Exam Worksheet found in Appendix 4 as well. You can also download a copy at profitoverproduction.com.

What to gather before you start your own Limited Financial Exam:

1. Balance sheet, run on a cash basis

2. Profit and loss statement, run on a cash basis for the same time frame as the balance sheet

3. Annual amounts paid toward any business debts you have (not including your building if you own it). You can calculate what you pay every month and multiply by twelve (or however many months you paid that year). Record any additional payments made.

4. Limited Financial Exam Worksheet found in Appendix 4

5. Pencil and highlighter

STEP ONE:

Starting with the profit and loss statement, highlight any expenses that directly benefit you as the owner. Obvious examples would be your salary and the associated payroll taxes, your health insurance, and retirement contributions. You may remember that it was more difficult to ascertain the total amount of owner's benefits using the "before" financials since the team and doctor payroll taxes were all lumped together. I used an asterisk in the figure below because only a portion of those payroll taxes belong to the owner's compensation.

Expenses	
Salary – Doctor	258,000
Taxes – Payroll	32,012*

Figure 4.3: Owner's Compensation on "Before" Financials

Other Expenses		
Owner Doctor Compensation		
Doctor Wages		150,000
Doctor Payroll Taxes		11,784
Doctor Health Insurance		13,217
Doctor Family Wages		12,210
Doctor Family Payroll Taxes		1,099
Total Owner Doctor Compensation	$	**188,310**

Figure 4.4: Owner's Compensation on "After" Financials

As mentioned in the last chapter, distributions are recorded on your balance sheet, toward the end of the statement. I have seen distributions labeled as "member's draw," "dividends," "owner's distributions," etc. If your distributions are further divided, for instance to taxes, student loan payments, or an owner's draw, *do not* highlight the tax distributions yet. If you're struggling to find the distributions on the "before" balance sheet, it's because none were taken and therefore none are recorded. Only record the personal distributions equal to $1,372 as part of the owner's compensation from the "after" balance sheet onto your LFE worksheet.

Equity	
Capital Stock	1,000
Retained Earnings	−143,078.00
Net Income	−3,096.00
Total Equity	$　　(145,174.00)

Figure 4.5: Equity Portion of Balance Sheet for POP, LLC, Before Cash Management

Equity	
Capital Stock	1,000
Retained Earnings	79,700.46
Distributions	
Personal	−1,372.49
Taxes	−83,435.97
Net Income	208,588.00
Total Equity	$ $ 204,480.00

Figure 4.6: Equity Portion of Balance Sheets for POP, LLC, After Cash Management

Transfer all the amounts associated with the highlighted expenses or distributions to the portion of the worksheet labeled "Owner's Compensation." You can see what this portion of the

LFE worksheet looks like for POP, LLC, below. If you are worried that the "after" owner's compensation is down close to $85,000 as compared to "before," there are a couple of things to consider. Originally, this dentist was contributing regularly to a 401(k) retirement plan and funding the profit-sharing portion when "extra" cash was available. Therefore, the pension company had the dentist run more money through payroll than is recommended as an "average" salary to maximize the difference in pay between the owner and the other high-wage employees. This dentist is no longer contributing funds to any retirement accounts and can therefore take less money out via payroll, while continuing to avoid triggering an audit since their wages are right at $150,000. This saves the owner the employer portion of the payroll taxes. Note that family wages are included in this calculation as they are a benefit exclusive to being an owner. Additionally, this dentist used distributions to pay estimated taxes directly from the business.

OWNER'S COMPENSATION CASH MANAGEMENT BEFORE | AFTER

	BEFORE	AFTER
Personal Distributions	None	$1,372
W-2 Wages	$258,000	$150,000
Doctor Payroll Taxes	$15,360	$11,784
Health Insurance	None	$13,217
Family Wages	None	$12,210
Family Payroll Taxes	None	$1,099
Retirement	**Right now it's not split up	None
TOTAL OWNER'S COMPENSATION	$273,360	$188,310

Figure 4.7: Owner's Compensation Portion of LFE Worksheet for POP, LLC, Before (L) and After (R) Cash Management

STEP TWO:

Now I want you to check for any distributions or expenses that your business paid toward *your* personal or business taxes. This does not include anything labeled as payroll taxes for you or your employees. This amount is often negligible—unless you have consistently taken out distributions to cover your estimated quarterly taxes or paid taxes on personal property. Record any distributions or non-payroll tax expenses on your LFE Worksheet. You will record a zero for the "before" LFE tax reserves, which is not unusual for someone who has not implemented Profit First. For the "after" LFE tax reserves, you will record the tax distribution amounts of $83,436 found on the balance sheet and $1,000 for the state PFE tax recorded on the P&L.

▷ **TAX RESERVES BEFORE | AFTER**

Tax Distributions	None	$83,436
Non-Payroll Taxes from P&L	None	$1,000
TOTAL TAX RESERVES	$0	$84,436

Figure 4.8: Tax Reserves Portion of LFE Worksheet POP, LLC,
for Before (L) and After (R) Cash Management

STEP THREE:

Your operating expenses—what most dentists refer to as "overhead"—are the most complicated to calculate, but we will start the same way we did with the other categories. Looking at your P&L, find the amount for "Total Expenses" and write it down on the "Overhead" section of your worksheet. Then add the amount of money you paid toward debt, including principal and interest, on the next line, as that money did indeed leave your account. If you are like me, you may not remember the amount you pay every month towards debt since it is most likely automatically withdrawn from your account. To calculate how much was paid, multiply one month's worth of debt payments towards long-term debt (practice, big equipment) by the number of months being evaluated (twelve if it's a full year). For POP, LLC, $80,627 was paid towards debt before cash management was implemented and since the practice was debt-free for the "after" period, no payments were made toward debt.

Record the total of any expenses you already attributed to owner dentist compensation or taxes. These are what I call "previously considered" expenses if you already recorded them on the LFE Worksheet *and* they were considered part of "Total Expenses" on your profit and loss statement. If you compare the "before" and "after" profit and loss statements, you will see that some of the non-cash expenses and owner's benefits are *not* included in the calculation of "Total Expenses" on the "after" financials; therefore, those items do *not* get subtracted from the expenses reported on the LFE. By this I mean that if any of those expenses were included in the total of expenses listed, you will need to record them here and subtract them from what's considered "overhead" as they are not technically considered operating expenses. If your owner's benefits or any non-payroll taxes are not included in the calculation for "Total Expenses," you will *not* subtract them here.

PROFIT AND LOSS STATEMENT Before Cash Management		
		TOTAL
Income		
Fee Income		963,051
Refunds		−16,690
Total Income	$	**946,361**
Expenses		
Accounting and Data Processing		67,288
Amortization Expense		31,828
Bank Charges		11,662
Business Promotion		10,646
Contract Labor		3,194
Contributions		3,450
Depreciation		7,304
Dues – Non-Deductible		200
Dues – Professional		4,503
Insurance – Operating		8,504
Interest Expense		18,022
Lab Costs		2,719
Legal and Professional		4,291
Meals and Entertainment		1,775
Meetings – Professional		750
Miscellaneous		332
Office Supplies and Expense		32,497
Professional Supplies		108,053
Rent		33,600
Repairs and Maintenance		495
Retirement Plan Expense		3,576
Safe Harbor Contribution		17,266
Salaries – Staff		262,922
Salary – Doctor		258,000
Taxes – Payroll		31,012

PROFIT AND LOSS STATEMENT Before Cash Management		
		TOTAL
Expenses (con't)		
Telephone		8,189
Training and Education		2,111
Travel and Conventions		11,561
Uniforms		2,142
Utilities		1,565
Total Expenses	$	**949,457**
NET INCOME	$	**(3,096)**

Figure 4.9: Total Expenses on the POP, LLC,
Before Cash Management Profit and Loss Statement

PROFIT AND LOSS STATEMENT After Cash Management		
		TOTAL
Total Expenses	$	**574,149**
NET OPERATING INCOME	$	**412,778**
Other Income		
Interest Income		114
Total Other Income	$	**114**
Other Expenses		
Owner Doctor Compensation		
Doctor Wages		150,000
Doctor Payroll Taxes		11,784
Doctor Health Insurance		13,217
Doctor Family Wages		12,210
Doctor Family Payroll Taxes		1,099
Total Owner Doctor Compensation	$	**188,310**
Amortization		0
Depreciation		15,994
Interest Expense		0

Total Other Expenses	$	204,304
NET OTHER INCOME	$	(204,190)

**Figure 4.10: Total Expenses on the POP, LLC,
After Cash Management Profit and Loss Statement**

Next, highlight any amortization, depreciation, or interest expenses, and record those numbers on the worksheet. If those values were *not* used in calculating the "Total Expenses," you will not write them down on this worksheet. If they *were* included as part of the "Total Expenses," you will need to subtract those non-cash expenses from your "New Expense Total."

The total in "Overhead" will be what you paid last year toward your daily operating expenses.

OVERHEAD

Total Expenses from P&L $949,457

Plus (+) Debt Payments $80,627

    New Expense Total $1,030,084

Subtract (-) Previously Considered

    Doctor W-2 Wages $258,000

    Doctor Payroll Taxes $15,360

    Other Doctor Benefits _____

    Taxes None

    Interest Expense $18,022

    Depreciation $7,304

    Amortization $31,828

TOTAL OVERHEAD $699,570

**Figure 4.11: Overhead Portion of the LFE Worksheet for POP, LLC,
Before Cash Management**

▷ **OVERHEAD**

Total Expenses from P&L	$574,149
Plus (+) Debt Payments	None
New Expense Total	$574,149

Subtract (-) Previously Considered

Doctor W-2 Wages _____

Doctor Payroll Taxes _____

Other Doctor Benefits _____

Taxes _____

Interest Expense _____

Depreciation _____

Amortization _____

TOTAL OVERHEAD	$574,149

Figure 4.12: Overhead Portion of the LFE Worksheet for POP, LLC, After Cash Management

STEP FOUR:

Before I explain how to calculate your profit, I want to remind you that there is such a thing as negative profit. I have been there, done that, and didn't even know it was possible. If you do the calculation for profit and find that yours is also negative, *you are in the right place* even if you start to feel uneasy. If you have a positive profit, I am going to help you evaluate whether it's "enough" and help you understand what leads to more profitability without having to produce more dentistry.

YOU ARE GOING TO LEARN HOW TO HAVE A MORE PROFITABLE PRACTICE.

Finally, the moment you have been waiting for: Let's calculate your profit. Use the number you found earlier under "Total Revenues." Subtract the following from your collections: owner dentist compensation, taxes, and overhead. The total—positive or negative—is your profit.

PROFIT

Total Income _____

Subtract (-)

    Owner's Compensation _____

    Tax Reserves _____

    Overhead _____

TOTAL PROFIT _____

Figure 4.13: Profit Calculation Formula

PROFIT

Total Income	$946,361
Subtract (-)	
Owner's Compensation	$273,360
Tax Reserves	None
Overhead	$699,570
TOTAL PROFIT	-$26,569

Figure 4.14: Profit Portion of the LFE Worksheet for POP, LLC, Before Cash Management

PROFIT

Total Income	$986,927
Subtract (-)	
Owner's Compensation	$188,310
Tax Reserves	$84,436
Overhead	$574,149
TOTAL PROFIT	$140,032

Figure 4.15: Profit Portion of the LFE Worksheet for POP, LLC, After Cash Management

STEP FIVE:

Now that we have our four big categories sorted, we need to calculate what percentage of your total collections they make up. This is what Mike Michalowicz refers to as the "current allocation percentages," or CAPs.[21] To do that, simply divide the subcategory amount by the total collections, then multiply by 100.

$$\frac{\text{Overhead}}{\text{Total Revenue}} \times 100 \quad = \quad \text{Overhead Percentage of Collections}$$

To calculate your Current Allocation Percentages (CAPs) for each account, simply divide each total by Total Income (aka Collections)

Example: Total Owner's Compensation of $200,000 divided by Total Income of $950,000 = 0.21 or 21%

▶ CURRENT ALLOCATION PERCENTAGES

$$\frac{\text{Owner's Compensation}}{\text{Total Income}} \times 100 \quad = \quad \underline{\hspace{3cm}}$$

$$\frac{\text{Tax Reserves}}{\text{Total Income}} \times 100 \quad = \quad \underline{\hspace{2cm}}$$

$$\frac{\text{Overhead}}{\text{Total Income}} \times 100 \quad = \quad \underline{\hspace{2cm}}$$

$$\frac{\text{Profit}}{\text{Total Income}} \times 100 \quad = \quad \underline{\hspace{2cm}}$$

Figure 4.16: How to Calculate Current Allocation Percentages (CAPs)

▷ CURRENT ALLOCATION PERCENTAGES

$$\frac{\text{Owner's Compensation}}{\text{Total Income}} \times 100 \quad = \quad \underline{\quad 29\% \quad}$$

$$\frac{\text{Tax Reserves}}{\text{Total Income}} \times 100 \quad = \quad \underline{\quad \text{None} \quad}$$

$$\frac{\text{Overhead}}{\text{Total Income}} \times 100 \quad = \quad \underline{\quad 74\% \quad}$$

$$\frac{\text{Profit}}{\text{Total Income}} \times 100 \quad = \quad \underline{\quad -3\% \quad}$$

Figure 4.17: CAP Worksheet for POP, LLC, Before Cash Management

▷ CURRENT ALLOCATION PERCENTAGES

$$\frac{\text{Owner's Compensation}}{\text{Total Income}} \times 100 \quad = \quad \underline{\quad 19\% \quad}$$

$$\frac{\text{Tax Reserves}}{\text{Total Income}} \times 100 \quad = \quad \underline{\quad 9\% \quad}$$

$$\frac{\text{Overhead}}{\text{Total Income}} \times 100 \quad = \quad \underline{\quad 58\% \quad}$$

$$\frac{\text{Profit}}{\text{Total Income}} \times 100 \quad = \quad \underline{\quad 14\% \quad}$$

Figure 4.18: CAP Worksheet for POP, LLC, After Cash Management

GENERAL DENTISTS SHOULD HAVE AN OVER-HEAD PERCENTAGE OF 65% OR LOWER. OVERHEAD FOR SPECIALISTS SHOULD BE 55% OR LOWER.

In Chapter 6, I will discuss in detail how to implement the Profit First cash management system into your practice. The basic premise is that you will increase your profitability by decreasing your overhead expenses by *slowly* and *incrementally* adjusting your Current Allocation Percentages. I am sharing the information about Target Allocation Percentages, or owners that still have long-term business liabilities and those that are debt-free, merely to introduce the concept of having goals or *targets* to work towards. Ideally, general dentists will have an overhead percentage less than 65% of collections and specialists should aim for an overhead of less than 55% of collections.

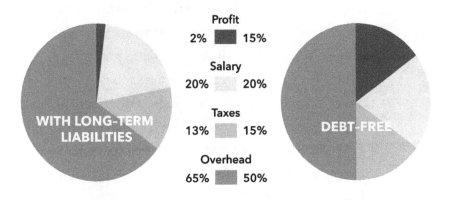

Figure 4.19: Target Allocation Percentages (TAPs) for Dentistry

▭——/⌚ SO, ARE YOU PROFITABLE ENOUGH?

I KNOW YOU PROBABLY NEED a break after having to use the calculator as much as you just did, but now you can quickly determine if you are profitable enough or if there is still more work to do to increase your profitability. I would like you to find three of the numbers you just evaluated to help summarize all you have learned in this chapter and get ready to go on to the next.

1. **Salary** – Are you paying yourself a market-based wage based on your location and days worked? Are you running that money through payroll? If so, well done. If not, is that because of your tax structure (not a designated S corporation)? If you aren't sure why you haven't paid yourself through payroll, or enough, then make sure it's on your list of questions to ask your accountant.

2. **Pretax Profit Percentage (PPP)** – Remember, 10% pretax profit is the new breakeven, so base your practice's financial wellness on that target. If yours is less, keep reading so you can learn how to increase profitability. If your PPP is greater than 15%, don't get too comfortable thinking it will always stay that high. Other dentists in town will start modeling your behaviors and are likely to gain some of the market share of patients, so keep reading to make sure you are doing everything to ensure and sustain predictable profitability.

3. **Profit reported on your Limited Financial Exam** – This should also be a minimum of 10%. Don't panic if it is below that number, as you will learn how to build a vault/cash reserve account, how to increase your tax basis, and how you can set aside enough money to invest in the new equipment or team members needed to grow your business without going into debt. I'm still right here with you. I've trailblazed the next steps ahead.

YOU ARE GOOD ENOUGH

You did it. You spent some time working *on* your business. You evaluated numbers and did some calculations. I know that even if you are shocked, embarrassed, or frustrated by what you found, you have what it takes to improve your profitability.

Remember, I once faced the harsh reality of looking at my numbers and finding that my profit was below zero. My practice wasn't on life support; it was coding, and I could hear people yelling "Clear!" as they applied the defibrillator. Depressing lunch breaks were spent in the quiet of my car, where I daydreamed of walking away and never looking back, but walking away wasn't an option. We needed the money. Plus, I was attached to my practice, my patients, and most importantly, my remaining team.

You don't have to do this alone. Many of your friends and colleagues have struggled to be profitable at one point or another. They will listen if you need to talk. Your team will support your mission to save your practice (and their jobs).

I highly encourage you to share with them that you are going to make it a priority to ensure the long-term success of your practice. If you aren't profitable enough *yet*, you will learn how to change that. Ideally, once you summit Profit Mountain, you will share what worked and any setbacks you experienced on your own journey to sustainable profitability.

CHAPTER 5
UNCOVER HIDDEN EXPENSES

When I first began working with colleagues to help them implement the Profit First cash management system, I quickly realized that the Limited Financial Exam was a great starting point, but I needed to analyze the numbers a little further. There was still something hidden within overhead's big number, "secrets" to be uncovered and included in the review.

Many dentists I spoke with did not know the "normal" target percentage for overhead until I shared that general dentists should aim for that percentage to be 65% of overall collections or lower, with specialists aiming for 55% of collections or lower spent on operating expenses. Even more confusing was exactly what operating expenses are included when people used the word "overhead." That's when I had my own aha moment and started evaluating how clients' expenditures compared to the industry standards for the most common expense categories within overhead: staff or team, rent and utilities, dental supplies, lab costs, office supplies, and marketing. Since I have a visual learning style preference, I knew that once I identified issues so that we could *see* what was making profits lower, those who learned like me would be able to find problems and fix them more readily.

Sometimes looking at things more deeply can be nerve-wracking, like when your operative professor peered through magnifying loupes at the preparation you submitted for your practical exam. I'm uneasy just thinking back to those days on the second floor of the UM-KC School of Dentistry. I absolutely dreaded turning in my mannikin for the faculty to grade. They always found fault with something since they could see my preparations in much greater detail using magnification. So as much as I hated to spend the money buying my own loupes as a dental student, I did it. Wearing them in the lab, I was able to see what the faculty saw and correct my mistakes before submitting anything to be graded. My attention to detail improved and my time spent worrying was minimized. I successfully graduated from the mannikin to real people down on the clinical floor, but I often tell people that if I had to repeat the second year of dental school, I wouldn't be a dentist.

Taking a closer look at your profit and loss statement will be the equivalent of putting on your loupes and suddenly seeing the margin that isn't quite right on your crown prep. You will gain one more critical piece of information needed to make the changes that ensure predictable profitability. And soon, you will be able to do the equivalent of submitting the perfect chamfer. Understanding what big expenses might be eating away at your profits is critical to your success.

You cannot fix an issue you cannot see.

HOW COMPARISON CAN BE HELPFUL

IN DENTAL SCHOOL, WE WERE taught not to worry about what everyone else was doing and stay in our lanes. We ignored that advice back then, since class standing did indeed matter for anyone considering a post-doc residency program. But I believe, as has often been said, that to stop *competing* with others, we must stop *comparing* ourselves, for "comparison is the thief of joy."[22]

This is one circumstance where comparing your business to others will help you, in this case to know if you are on the right track in terms of your business health and specifically your spending patterns. Sometimes only looking at overhead expenses as a whole hides the secrets that the six most common expense numbers will reveal upon closer inspection. Much like a dental radiograph shows more about the extent of decay—which cannot always be determined when looking at a tooth in the mouth—analyzing these numbers allows you to see exactly where you are spending more than is the norm. Strategic change can then be initiated.

Small changes lead to big wins.

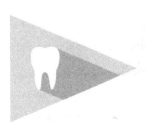

IF YOU ARE UNSURE HOW TO GENERATE A REPORT SHOWING THESE EXPENSES AS PERCENTAGES OF COLLECTIONS, YOU CAN ASK YOUR ACCOUNTANT TO GENERATE ONE FOR YOU.

THE "BIG SIX" EXPENSES

I CALCULATED THE AVERAGE RANGE of the percentage of collections for the expenses presented below after I reviewed online dental articles and blog posts and spoke with my dental accountants and colleagues, and I confirmed these averages when I reviewed financial reports generated by different dental-specific CPA firms.

You will soon know how to break the code, to reveal all the hidden secrets that can be found within your big overhead number. I'll discuss the expenditures related to each subcategory, as well as what to do if you are outside of the average range. Overall, you want to be in range or below; however, sometimes coming in below range might indicate you aren't spending enough. This could simply be because you are currently short-staffed or haven't spent money on business promotion recently since you are already at capacity in terms of scheduling new patients.

Time to adjust your loupes or, better yet, show off your X-ray vision. Let's uncover the hidden "decay" that's eating away at your profit.

1. Staff or Team Expenses: 23–27% of collections

Most of your operating expenses will be spent paying your supporting staff members. Later in the book, I'll discuss more about your team, what makes it good, how you can make it better, what to do if your employees are costing you too much, etc. For now, I want to keep this as simple as possible. Staff expenses include wages, payroll taxes, health insurance, and any retirement contributions you make for employees in your office, as well as any temporary workers. Do *not* include what you pay associates or any other dentists in your practice unless you have an associate doing hygiene regularly.

If you are spending less than the target range, perhaps it's because you are a general dentist who is short a part-time hygienist, so you're covering some of the prophy appointments. It may also be because your team isn't being paid enough. I will discuss later how to evaluate whether your team members are properly compensated. If they are not, you risk having higher rates of turnover and/or attracting less capable employees. The authors of *The E-Myth Dentist* invite you to ask yourself, "What's more important: saving money, or building the best team you can to provide the highest quality of care to your patients?"[23]

If you're on the high side of staff reimbursement, *you are not alone!* Even before the worker shortage, most dentists whose practices I evaluated were spending too much on their employees' compensation. This was primarily because they didn't even know how much they were spending, and they didn't know what the "normal" range was. The year I implemented Profit First, my team expenses were almost 43%! Within a year they were down to 41%, and down to 33% within five years, which is still considered high. Remember Dr. Reynolds, from earlier in the book? Her staff was getting 50% of collections. If your payroll is too high, it's time to evaluate whether you have too many staff or if their wages and benefits are higher than they should be to be competitive. Are you outsourcing jobs that people on your staff should have plenty of time to do? Could you take back some of the administrative responsibilities and eliminate a position up front?

2. Facilities and Rent: 5–9% of collections

This expense includes rent, utilities, janitorial services, maintenance, and the monthly monitoring service for your security system. If you own your office space, you should be paying rent to a separate business entity for your building that more than covers your principal and interest on the mortgage. If you currently pay this mortgage directly from your dental business bank account, I suggest you speak with your accountant about the IRS regulations concerning a lease agreement between your dental business and a business entity for your building. Make sure you are paying yourself a rental rate comparable to the going rate per square foot in your city.

If these expenses are too high, it could mean your collections aren't high enough to warrant having as much space as you currently do. You will need to increase revenue, renegotiate at lease renewal, or even consider moving your office space. If you are spending less than the average, you can consider expanding your space or just celebrating that you chose well in terms of your office size and location.

3. Dental Supplies: 5–10% of collections

These are the disposable clinical supplies used every day when you see patients, things like gloves, masks, gauze, anesthetic, bonding agents, prophy paste, etc. It does not include any dental *equipment* that may have been purchased from a supplier at the same time, so make sure you alert your accountant to any equipment purchases. Also, do not include any true office supplies in this category, as they are an expense of their own. For surgical practices like mine, you can include bone graft materials, membranes, and implants as part of your dental supply costs. Just know you will likely be on the high end of the average range.

Thankfully, none of us has to rely on purchasing from the big three dental supply companies to take care of our disposable dental product needs. With more competition in the market, overall, the costs have come down. You can now ask your colleagues online, in groups like Nifty Thrifty Dentists, where to find the best deals. Additionally, there are paid dental groups, like the Official Mommy Dentists in Business group, where a perk of membership is not only receiving a better price on supplies but also being able to get your hands on items that might be in short supply, such as N-95 masks at the beginning of the COVID-19 pandemic.

If you find you don't have the time to do the bargain-hunting on your own or the team member assigned to ordering doesn't search out the best deals, you should consider using a company like Method Procurement, which analyzes costs of supplies and lets you know the best places to order from. Chris Sands of Pro-Fi 20/20 Dental CPAs recommends this to his clients, and his accounting firm has seen a reduction in their bottom line of 1–2%. When I asked him to explain further, he said, "If supply expenses were 7% of collections, then that expense would decrease to 6%, or even 5%, of collections." This tool has been especially helpful for some of my clients given the way costs are rising due to inflation.

4. Lab Expenses: 4–10% of collections

When analyzing financials, I have found that the expenditure on lab costs has the widest range in terms of the percentage of revenue. For surgical, pediatric, or endodontics practices, this expense should be very low. General dentists making in-house restorations (CEREC crowns, for example) should also be on the low end in terms of lab expenditures, although the materials needed to fabricate the restorations should be considered part of these expenses. Offices moving teeth with clear aligners, cosmetic practitioners, or prosthodontists who are doing bigger cases that involve some type of lab-fabricated replacement will naturally have higher lab bills.

As you likely already know, all labs are not the same. You must not sacrifice quality for a better deal. However, if the difference in quality is negligible, use the lab with lower costs. Keep in mind that if you have to send back crowns—or even if you don't have to send them back but must spend more chair time on adjustments—it is ultimately costing you.

RULE OF THUMB: CHARGE 4-5X THE LAB FEE FOR THE RESTORATION.

5. Marketing and Business Promotion: 3–8% of collections

In all the financial reviews I have done, I have yet to see anyone spend up to 8% on marketing or business promotion. That said, a quick internet search shows it is recommended that *all* businesses spend between 7–12% of revenue on marketing. When I began my journey to more predictable profit, I was shocked to learn that I was supposed to be spending so much on marketing. In the intervening years, it has made more sense to me.

For your practice to be successful in the long run, you must have consistent revenue. And that will not come solely through seeing your well-maintained patients of record because eventually, they won't need lots of dentistry. Plus, even if you are the most beloved dentist in your area, you will experience a natural attrition of patients. People change jobs or insurance companies. They move or die. It's part of life. You will need new patients and, more importantly, you will need patients who have dental needs you can fulfill with your amazing skills. The only way to make sure those people keep calling your office and showing up for new patient exams is to attract, market to, or advertise to them. They need to know you exist and why they should come to see *you.* You can find some great ideas on how to set yourself apart in another book by Mike Michalowicz, *Get Different!*[24]

I do *not* want you to spend an extravagant amount of money on a new webpage, mailers, or even a social media expert. It *would* be wise to figure out how to reach the kind of people you want to attract—your ideal patients—and spend some money promoting your business to them. If you are a pediatric dentist, you might spend time and money advertising at local sports fields or practice facilities. You might sponsor your own kid's basketball team and have them wear shirts with your logo on them. Maybe you'll spend some money on lunch-and-learns with referring dental offices or even pediatricians in your zip code. Unless you are booked out solid for weeks, you likely need to spend more on business promotion than you are currently.

6. Office Supplies: 1–3% of collections

Items to include in this category are all the expenses associated with running the "front" or nonclinical part of the practice: Post-it notes, letterhead, envelopes, pens, ink cartridges for the printers, toilet paper, etc.

Don't overlook this small expense. Remember, when my office supply expense was 3.5%, it was a major red flag to my bookkeeper. It is now 1%, which is where it typically runs for my office. By knowing what the average should be, and recognizing that my expenses were entirely too high, we were able to identify that my ex-employee, Stacie, was stealing from me.

You might be surprised what kinds of supplies walk out of your office. Kessler International, known as a leader in forensic accounting, surveyed 500 retail and service industry employees. Over half of the respondents, 52% of the workers, copped to stealing office supplies.[25] If your practice has total annual collections of $750,000 and you catch someone stealing 1% of your annual revenue in supplies—either for themselves or to resell—that is $7,500 that could have been in your profit account.

ALL THE OTHER MISCELLANEOUS EXPENSES

THE SIX KEY EXPENSES ACCOUNT for roughly 45–60% of all your overhead expenditures, but there will still be more money leaving your office to cover the miscellaneous expenses I haven't listed in any of the other categories. These include, but are not limited to, licenses, dues and subscriptions, continuing education courses and travel, meals, computer maintenance, accounting services, and other professional fees.

The point to keep in mind is that if you are a general dentist, you want all your operating expenses, aka overhead, to be less than 65% of your collections. Specialists' overhead should be even less. When I first began working with dentists as clients, I noticed that there were far fewer specialists reaching out for help with implementing Profit First. There are more general dentists than specialists, but even so, the difference was noticeable. Spoiler alert: If I were forced to go back through dental school and residency and had to choose a specialty based solely on potential profitability in private practice, periodontics would *not* be where I ended up. So far, I'm thinking I would invest in counseling to overcome my anxiety about performing root canals and become an endodontist—although it's quite possible the therapy would end up costing more in the end. Wink wink.

KPIs OF OVERHEAD

STAFF	SUPPLIES	LAB FEES	RENT/FACILITIES	MARKETING
23–27%	5–10%	4–10%	5–9%	3–8%
Wages	Disposables for Clinical Dentistry	Lab Costs	Rent	Business Promotion
Payroll Taxes		Clear Aligner Fees	Utilities	Website Development
Health Insurance		Supplies for In-house Restorations	Repairs	
Outsourced Jobs			Maintenance to Your Space	Internal Marketing Costs
Temp Help				
				Mailers

Figure 5.1: Dental Averages for Expenses

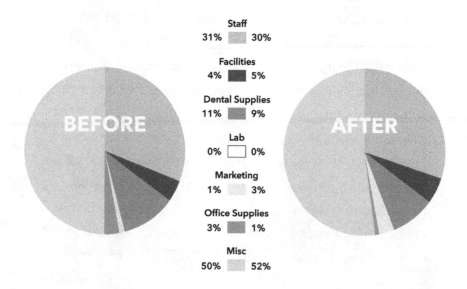

	Before	After
Staff	31%	30%
Facilities	4%	5%
Dental Supplies	11%	9%
Lab	0%	0%
Marketing	1%	3%
Office Supplies	3%	1%
Misc	50%	52%

Figure 5.2: Expense Percentages for POP, LLC,
Before and After Cash Management

Looking at Figure 5.2, which shows the "before" and "after" percentages of the big expenses, you can see that one of the highest main expenses was for staff (the team), and that both the lab and marketing expenses were on the low side. While the "after" pie graph does show decreases in team, supply, and office expenses, there was a slight increase in the rent and facilities category and in marketing. You may be wondering how an overall change of "only" 2% in these expenses helped this practice owner change their profitability so much. For one thing, 2% of close to a million dollars is a sizeable amount of money. Plus, the dentist paid extra toward debt and eliminated all long-term liabilities. That increased profitability significantly, as the annual debt payments were close to 9% of the collections before. Those two changes helped the dentist decrease the overhead allocation percentage from 74% to 58%. Once dentists have paid off all their long-term liabilities, it's certainly possible to get overhead closer to 55%, or even lower for specialists.

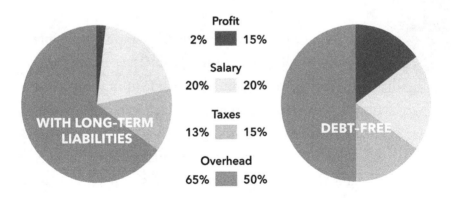

Figure 5.3: Target Allocation Percentages (TAPs) of Collections with and without Long-Term Liabilities

HOW TO CHANGE THE PERCENTAGES IN YOUR FAVOR

ABOVE, I GAVE A FEW suggestions within each category for what to consider if you need to decrease expenses. I also promised to talk more about teams later. Getting back to the big picture, there are only two ways to change the expense percentages in your favor.

To change the expense percentages
in your favor, increase collections, decrease
expenses, or do both simultaneously
for the most benefit.

1. Increase Collections

The "produce more to make more" mantra does apply here if you actually collect more, too. The one caveat is that you must maintain your costs while producing more. Examples of how to do this include decreasing the amount of chair time for each procedure; utilizing block scheduling to make sure the appropriate number of income-producing procedures are done each day; and adding services to hygiene appointments, such as dental radiographs or fluoride. If you want to jump ahead to Chapter 7, you can learn more about those specific examples.

Some other ways to increase revenue are to go out of network, increase your fees, and make sure your accounts receivables are up-to-date. I expand on these, and other related topics, in Chapter 8.

2. Decrease Expenses

The obvious way to decrease expenses is to spend less money. What's not so obvious is how to find exactly where you are overspending. Are your hygienists paid too much? Are you overstaffed? Are all your dental supplies from one company rather than various suppliers that offer lower prices for the items you need? Do you have a good inventory system?

The other sneaky way to decrease expenses is by decreasing the amount available to spend on expenses by, wait for it … taking profit first. In the next chapter, I will explain the rationale and psychology that underscore why this works. But for now, just know that if you take your profit first, you will leave less money in your Overhead account and will therefore be forced to spend less, as you can only use what's available in that account for your expenses.

Sales - Profit = Expenses

In the next chapter, I will share the Profit First dental "pearls" I have discovered over the years and how I apply them to my own business. This will include the best and most predictable way to spend less on expenses (lower your overhead expense percentage) and figure out where you need to "trim the fat." You will also learn the tweaks that I think make the cash management system more user-friendly for dentists and the nitty-gritty details of setting up your bank accounts so you can get the system up and running.

YOU ARE ABOVE AVERAGE!

YOU REMEMBER THE OLD JOKE they used to crack in dental school, right? You know the one ...

"What do you call the last person in your dental class?"

"Doctor."

Ha ha. Yet, it's true. If you pass all the requirements to graduate as well as your written and clinical boards, you will most likely get to practice in the state of your choosing, proudly display your diplomas, and answer to the title of "Doctor." No one will ask to see your resumé or your grade card. They may not even know where you went to dental school.

No matter how your expenses compare to those of your colleagues, YOU are above average! You know how I know? Because you have already made it through five chapters of a book dedicated to the business side of dentistry. You didn't let the fact that you prefer doing dentistry to reading a business book deter you. You invested time out of the operatory to learn how to have a more predictably profitable business. You made time to work *on* your practice. Last, but certainly not least, you looked at your numbers. Then you took an even closer look. Not only is that intimidating because it involves math and calculations, but it's also emotional because one of our biggest fears is that we aren't good enough. We get so caught up worrying about what we might find, we just don't look—or at least, I didn't. However, by taking a closer look, you can gauge your progress and adjust as necessary.

You, yes *you*, have done all the things. You have the information you need to move on down your own yellow brick road to profitability and keep heading up Profit Mountain. Yes, yes, I did just work in a *Wizard of Oz* reference. I'm a Kansan. It's practically a requirement.

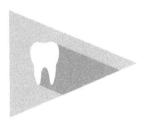

The work you did in this chapter allowed you to finalize your diagnosis (sick practice) and treatment plan (remove the decay that is eating away at your profit). It's time to remove disease and restore health to your business. This is the moment you have been waiting for, when you get to show off all the skills you learned in dental school. You already know how to sequence treatment and follow the appropriate steps to restore teeth and mouths to health. The next step is to implement a cash management system in your practice. This protocol will allow you to restore financial health to your practice and use your normal behavior—checking your bank balances—to help you make better budgeting decisions.

CHAPTER 6
IMPLEMENT CASH MANAGEMENT

To get the most comprehensive instructions and information on the Profit First cash management system, I will always refer you to Mike Michalowicz's original *Profit First: Transform Your Business from a Cash-Eating Monster to a Money-Making Machine.*[26] Many of you have asked me to write the simplified dental version in language you can better understand; therefore, I have included what I refer to as "Profit First Post-It Note Pearls" in this chapter. This essential information will give you a basic understanding of how using a cash management system can transform your practice. I have also included the nitty-gritty details of what you need to do at the bank to get this system up and running in your practice without feeling overwhelmed or discouraged.

While "pearls" from continuing education courses are usually limited to a couple of big-picture takeaway points, this chapter looks at the big picture as well as the minutiae that might confuse you. We are going to move away from math for a while and delve into history and psychology, then move on to methodology and action steps. There is a little bit of something for everyone. While I am more than happy to follow another successful business owner's path, I still have the desire to know *why* I am taking those particular steps and how they might benefit my progression. I also want to know *why* it is imperative that I do them—or, in other words, what bad outcome might happen if I choose to do things my way. And finally, I want to know *why* some steps might be slightly different because I am a dentist. You probably feel the same way.

THE EVOLUTION OF CASH MANAGEMENT

USING CASH ENVELOPES TO HELP people track and budget their personal money existed well before Dave Ramsey brought the concept mainstream with his book *Total Money Makeover*.[27] My favorite star in the current cash envelope system space is "The Budget Mom."[28] I am a longtime subscriber to her weekly newsletter, have utilized many of her "freebies," and even purchased and utilized her Budget by Paycheck® boxed set to track my family's personal expenses, retirement, and investment growth. I have since switched to a more comprehensive online version of cash management, working with Chris Sands and his Provider Planning financial management group. Many financial planners and banks have different programs and software available to help their clients with the fundamentals of personal cash management.

In terms of bringing the system over to the business side, I credit Mike Michalowicz. When people ask me exactly what *Profit First* is about, I explain it as the business version of a cash envelope system, where businesses utilize bank accounts as opposed to cash envelopes. This is what Mike refers to as "bank balance accounting," in which we base our spending decisions on the money available in our bank accounts instead of reviewing our financial statements (as traditional financial accounting methodology would have us do).[29] Mike's method is easier and more convenient, as most of us have our bank information readily available to us, even on our smartphones.

"Bank balance accounting" refers to the natural tendency for us to check our bank balance(s) and spend accordingly.

The basic premise of any "cash" budgeting system is that you divide your income into different spending categories: home mortgage, groceries, entertainment, and so on. You or your accountant do a review of your historical spending patterns so you can use that information to set a monthly spending allowance for each category. That amount of money is then placed in a literal envelope. The only money spent on purchases from that category must come from within the designated envelope. The aim is to prevent you from overspending by limiting what is available for you to spend. The Profit First methodology modernized this tried-and-true system by bringing it to the business realm and utilizing bank accounts in place of cash envelopes.

The psychology of why this works relates to Parkinson's Law of human behavior. Parkinson's Law states that "Our demand upon a resource tends to expand to match the supply of that resource."[30] In short, if we have more funds available to make a purchase, we will use more funds. To illustrate the concept in *Profit First*, Mike Michalowicz uses an example of a tube of toothpaste.[31] When you have a brand-new tube of toothpaste, you don't worry too much about the amount you squeeze out onto your toothbrush. However, over time, as less and less toothpaste remains in the tube, you become more and more mindful of how much you use per brushing activity and quite creative about getting the last smidge out of the tube.

When I talk about Parkinson's Law with colleagues, I use toilet paper as my example, since the pandemic made it all too clear what can happen when supplies run low. Pre-pandemic, there were no supply chain disruptions to speak of and toilet paper was readily available. When you opened a brand-new roll of "good" toilet paper, you didn't worry about how many squares you used each time you frequented the restroom. However, at the beginning of the COVID-19 pandemic, there was a rush on grocery stores and big box retail outlets. Toilet paper was one of the first commodities unavailable for purchase. Shelves were bare. Even the cheap stuff was gone. People got nervous and began to hoard their stashes of toilet paper, using it sparingly. I left a minimal amount of toilet paper at the office and took the remaining rolls home in case we needed them during the forced shutdown period. Both of my behaviors—using less of the available toilet paper *and* getting creative with where I might source more toilet paper—perfectly illustrate why the concept of Parkinson's Law can be so beneficial for us as business owners.

We can use Parkinson's Law of human behavior to our advantage when implementing a cash management system. By allocating funds to different spending categories, we are forced to adjust and use only what money remains, as well as get creative with funding or finding other resources.

PARKINSON'S LAW DICTATES THAT AS AVAILABLE FUNDS DECREASE, OUR SPENDING WILL TOO.

JULIE'S POST-IT NOTE PEARLS

I HAVE BEEN MAILING OUT *Profit First* books for years, with Post-it notes included where I want readers to pay particular attention. The very first one addresses the question, "Does more revenue mean you are more successful?" My Post-it note says, "NO! I am so sick of people telling me to produce more." The following are my Post-it Note Pearls regarding the implementation of this cash management system in your dental practice.

USE MULTIPLE BANK ACCOUNTS

ONE OF THE NEXT NOTES reads, "Yes, you really need all the bank accounts."

I never considered not opening the bank accounts because I tend to follow rules, to-do lists, and action steps from those who have gone before. However, once I started helping colleagues implement the system, it was the task of opening additional accounts that triggered the "Do I have to?" comments. I explained that for the system to work as intended, maximizing Parkinson's Law when we base our spending on what we see in our bank account, then the information must be readily accessible via looking at our bank account balances and *not* after opening up a spreadsheet and trying to remember if we updated the categories correctly. If looking at spreadsheets, financial statements, or budgets worked, you wouldn't be reading this book.

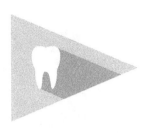

IF LOOKING AT SPREADSHEETS, FINANCIAL STATEMENTS, OR BUDGETS WORKED, YOU WOULDN'T BE READING THIS BOOK.

ALLOCATE MONEY ONCE PER WEEK

In *Profit First,* Mike suggests allocating funds according to the 10/25 rule, which dictates that you only move money on the 10th and 25th of each month.[32] Even though I'm an avid rule follower, this one never seemed to work for me. What happens if the 10th falls on a Sunday? What if there isn't enough money in the Overhead account when I need to run payroll, but it's only because of a timing issue? I quickly found that most dentists need to allocate funds more often because we receive incoming funds almost daily. Not only do we receive funds for services provided each day we are open, we also receive direct deposits from insurance companies, credit card processing companies, etc.

Since I do think it's important to notice changes in your "normal" income levels, I suggest that dentists allocate money from their Income account into their various holding accounts once a week. This should be done on the same day every week whether you are working in the office or not. You get to choose what day is best for you and your practice. You merely need to be consistent.

I chose "Money Mondays" to allocate funds. I move money from my Income account to the other accounts as soon as I come in to work that day. It gives me something to look forward to every Monday morning, and most days I feel like I hit the jackpot when I see the Profit account increase. Conversely, if the available income to disperse is lower than most weeks, I immediately know adjustments need to be made during the upcoming week (for example: add patient appointments, call about unpaid claims, or collect on outstanding account receivables).

Many bank holidays fall on Mondays, but I can still transfer funds online when the bank is closed. Also, it's very rare that I'm out of the office on a Monday, so it works well for me. If you take an administrative day on Wednesdays, you might choose to move your money then. Just remember to be consistent. Learn the patterns of your collections. Respond appropriately if the weekly collection amount is lower than normal.

REWARD YOURSELF

REWARDS ARE POWERFUL FOR THOSE of us who chose dentistry as a profession. We are perfectionists at heart and love to get things right, down to the millimeter-or-less level. Many of us are goal-driven, but we are not always patient. If we cannot reach perfection immediately, we do need to see significant progress quickly. The best way to feel differently from the get-go is to reward yourself for implementing this system. At the end of the first quarter of implementation, it is *imperative* that you use at least some of the funds in your Profit account for something *you* want.

Reward yourself for making progress

You might not be able to afford a fancy weekend away with your family, a new purse, or even the latest smartphone on the market, but you will have some money you can use to treat yourself. If you have implemented the system, you will, at the very least, have 1% of the income collected that quarter available to spend. So do something to treat yo'self right! No guilt attached. Enjoy this first taste of progress on your steady climb up Profit Mountain. Before you know it, you will be attaching your flag to the summit.

MAKE MONTHLY ADJUSTMENTS

IF YOU ARE CONSISTENTLY ENDING each month with extra money remaining in your Overhead account, then you aren't exactly allowing Parkinson's Law to work for you. You shouldn't change the actual allocation percentage until a new quarter rolls around, but you will need to move some of the excess money into your Profit account after adjusting for upcoming bills and payroll that need to be paid during the week. Keep in mind, once money goes into the Profit account, it does not come back out until quarterly distributions are made.

If you have a monthly surplus in your Overhead account, move money into your Profit account

HAVE REGULAR CHECKUPS

CONSIDER THESE THE EQUIVALENT OF your periodontal maintenance appointments. Ideally, you will conduct—or have someone else conduct—a Limited Financial Examination every three to four months. You will review your financial diagnosis and evaluate any numbers that need more attention. If you consistently have a surplus in your Overhead account, you will decrease your overhead allocation percentage by 1-3% in any given quarter. If you try to do more than that, it will be too much, too soon. A slow and steady uphill progression up Profit Mountain will ultimately get you there quicker and without any "injuries."

Conduct a quarterly Limited Financial Exam and adjust your allocation percentages

ACCOUNTABILITY

As WHEN YOU BEGIN TO eat differently, cut back on alcohol, or make plans to exercise more regularly, you need to let those around you know. Not only can they help (or hinder) your progress, they also can be your biggest cheerleaders or, at the very least, the true friends and trusted advisors who will keep you on task in your moments of weakness. Find another dentist who is using this money management method and commit to texting each other every week once you've moved your money. Promise each other that you will reach out if you find you can't make payroll and want to "temporarily" move money from the Profit or Tax accounts to cover the missing funds. You might also consider signing up for ongoing support from a Profit First Professional, like me, with whom you can check in regularly as questions arise. Believe me, I love to celebrate when the profits are rolling in, but I also enjoy hearing about how you avoided crisis mode.

Be accountable

NITTY-GRITTY BANK ACCOUNT DETAILS

FOR ALL THE ABOVE-MENTIONED POST-IT Note Pearls to work, you will need additional bank accounts to hold money. What is paid for out of each account will be covered shortly, but first I want to remind you of the importance of working with a supportive bank. You need a bank and banker that can help make your vision—to get your cash management under control and maximize profits by utilizing multiple holding accounts—a reality. It only makes sense if that can be accomplished without incurring costs for adding accounts or dealing with minimum balance requirements.

Before you go on the hunt for a new bank where you can open all your new accounts, consider working with your existing bank, especially if you already have a relationship with someone there. It makes the transition so much easier if you have an established connection with a banker. When I told my local bankers what I wanted and how I would like the accounts to be set up, they thought it over and obliged. I now have nine accounts with them for my periodontal practice, even though I no longer *have to* now that my business loans are all paid off.

You can edit the following email with your own information to use as a starting point with your bank. To download an editable document, visit drjuliewoods.com.

To Whom It May Concern

Re: **Opening New Bank Accounts**

After reading *Profit Over Production* by Dr. Julie C. Woods, I have decided to implement the profit first cash management system. This system was first introduced in the book *Profit First* by Mike Michalowicz (2014). Since then, numerous businesses have successfully implemented the program.

I will need to open several new bank accounts. Most of these accounts will act as holding accounts with one being dedicated to paying most of the operating expenses of the dental practice. *Ideally, there would be no minimum balance requirements or extra fees associated with opening these accounts.*

I will need one additional *checking* account labeled **Overhead** and four *savings* accounts labelled: **Profit, Owner's Comp, Tax Reserves** and **Vault**. Money will be transferred into the new accounts approximately once per week (from the INCOME account – the existing business account).

I will need online access to make the transfers easily. Please enable the bill pay feature for the Overhead account as well.

Sincerely,

Future Profit First Dentist

Figure 6.1: Example Email to Banker

ACCOUNTS

AS THE ABOVE SAMPLE EMAIL says, you will want to set up (at minimum) the following *new* accounts:

1. Profit, Tax, and Owner's Compensation. These accounts work best as savings accounts since money will leave them less than six times per month in total. If you already have additional money in savings, you won't necessarily need to open a Vault account; however, if you don't have one, I highly recommend you open one at the same time. Adjust the email to your banker according to your needs.

2. One checking account, your new Overhead account. You will need to move any automatic debt payment withdrawals to this account. Additionally, you will need to adjust any other auto-payments, such as to dental suppliers, credit card companies, your mobile phone company, etc., so they come out of this account. You will want to evaluate any other recurring payments individually to ensure that they are for products or services you really need. If not, cut the expenses. When I set up this new account, I did not order any checks, even though this is the main account through which money leaves my practice. I pay as much as I can on my business credit card, which earns me points for travel, and use the online bill-pay feature of the Overhead checking account for anything I cannot pay with a credit card. Make sure your bank sets up online bill-pay for you

and gives you online access to all the other accounts so you can easily see all of them under one login and readily transfer funds between them.

ACCOUNTS	KIND OF ACCOUNT
Income*	Checking
Profit	Savings
Owner's Compensation	Savings
Tax	Savings
Overhead	Checking

Figure 6.2: Accounts Needed

*Use existing deposit account

PREPARING FOR ALLOCATION DAY

ONCE THE ACCOUNTS ARE SET up and all auto-withdrawals have been changed over, you are ready for the final preparations necessary before your first allocation day. Find the current allocation percentages (CAPs) that you calculated in Chapter 4. These are the percentages you will use to start your climb up Profit Mountain, and you will want to have the numbers handy when you go online to label your accounts. In my online banking portal, under the profile setting tab, I can label the accounts *and* change the order in which they appear on the screen. I hope you can do the same.

LABEL YOUR ACCOUNTS ONLINE

First, label your existing business account "Income." This is the account through which all money derived from seeing patients flows into your practice. Other than credit card processing fees and occasional overpayment refunds to patient credit cards, no money from this account should leave the business.

Next, find the new checking account and label it "Overhead." Make sure to include the CAP you will use this quarter as part of the name, for example, "Overhead CAP 72%." Label the three remaining saving accounts for Profit, Tax, and Owner's Compensation, making sure to include the CAP in the tagline for each. Remember, CAPs are your current allocation percentages of total collections. It's important to include the number as part of your label so you remember what percentage of income to move to each account on allocation day.

NEW ACCOUNT LABELS

Income
Profit CAP 12%
Owner's Compensation CAP 15%
Tax CAP 5%
Overhead CAP 78%

Figure 6.3: Example List of Labeled Bank Accounts (with CAPs)

If you can order your accounts, I would like you to put them in the following order: Income, Profit, Owner's Compensation, and Tax, with Overhead at the very bottom of the list. This is so that we can use "the primacy effect," another behavioral principle, in our favor.[33] The gist of the principle is, our brains focus on what we see first. It's one of the reasons first impressions are so important.

Below is a list of words describing a tuh-MAY-toe versus a tuh-MAH-toe. I want you to glance at the words and, as quickly as possible, decide whether you'd prefer a tuh-MAY-toe or a tuh-MAH-toe. Here you go:

1. TASTY, FLAVORFUL, RIPE, JUICY, MESSY, CHEWY
2. CHEWY, MESSY, JUICY, RIPE, TASTY, FLAVORFUL

Know which one you prefer? Unless tomatoes cause an inflammatory response in your body and you don't prefer either one, I'm guessing you chose tuh-MAY-toe, aka option one, because who doesn't love a tasty, flavorful bite of food? However, if you were paying close attention, you noticed that both sets of words are the same, just in a different sequence. The striking difference, other than the pronunciation, is that the order in which the traits are presented is more appetizing in #1 than in #2. That's why, if your Profit account is the first thing you see after your Income account, you will focus on it the most. It won't be forgotten. You will make sure that account grows.

Words matter. And this is why the "first" part of Profit First matters.

ALLOCATION DAY

As I MENTIONED PREVIOUSLY, I allocate income to the various accounts on Money Mondays, first thing in the morning. Once you get used to this process, it will take you less than a minute to move the money. Remember, I have nine different accounts for my periodontal practice—and I can complete the task that quickly.

First, you need to see how much money is sitting in your Income account. Things to note: Do you see roughly the same amount in the account every week when you move money on the same day? If the number is lower this week, why? Were you out on vacation last week? Was there a bank holiday? Did you forget to send statements to patients who owe balances? If it's higher than usual, you still want to know why. Were there prepayments for upcoming services? Did you finally receive insurance payments for some unpaid claims? If possible, you want to try to re-create those kinds of weeks.

Before you move any money, decide how much of a buffer you need to leave in the Income account to cover any unexpected withdrawals, such as patient overpayment refunds or similar withdrawals on overpayments made by insurance companies you are in network with. I tend to leave about $5,000 in my Income account, but you can certainly choose a higher or lower amount, depending on your comfort level.

Now that you know the total amount of funds you plan to allocate, you can figure out exactly how much needs to be moved into each account by multiplying the total amount to be moved by the corresponding CAP for each account. For example, if you have $20,000 to allocate this week and 72% needs to go into the Overhead account, you will use the following formula:

$$\$20{,}000 \times 0.72 = \$14{,}400$$

Initiate an online transfer of $14,400 from your Income account to your Overhead account. Then repeat the process with the remaining accounts and their labeled allocation percentages.

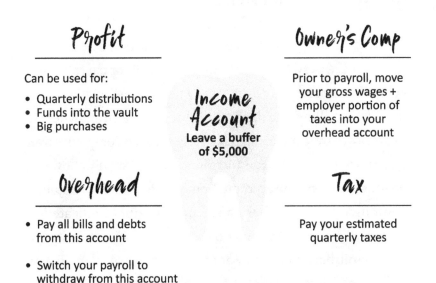

Profit

Can be used for:

- Quarterly distributions
- Funds into the vault
- Big purchases

Income Account

Leave a buffer of $5,000

Owner's Comp

Prior to payroll, move your gross wages + employer portion of taxes into your overhead account

Overhead

- Pay all bills and debts from this account

- Switch your payroll to withdraw from this account

Tax

Pay your estimated quarterly taxes

Figure 6.4: Allocation Day

I did it this way for almost four years, then finally created the "Profit First Dental Tool," which utilizes the features of an Excel spreadsheet to quickly determine the percentages for *all* the accounts. My clients merely need to put in the total amount of income to be dispersed and the calculations are done for them. With one entry, they know exactly what amount of money to move into each account.

Once you have moved all the money, you can also quickly initiate bill payments via the online bill-pay feature. That way, you limit such activity to only once per week, too. If money is moved and bills that must be paid with a check are initiated, it's time to log off until the following week and/or it's time to fund payroll.

PREPARING FOR PAYROLL

ONE OF THE FIRST THINGS I did when I took over ownership of my practice was switch over to direct deposit for payroll, and I highly recommend you do the same. I try to do as much online as possible as it allows me the flexibility to do it from anywhere in the world, at any time of day. I have used several companies over the years to process payroll and found that most only allow you to withdraw from one account. Some Profit First Professionals recommend that you have a separate account dedicated to payroll, and one of my own holding accounts is dedicated to staff payroll, but I still don't want to lump my own salary in with staff wages. I like to see that I am taking out the appropriate percentage of collections for myself and not overpaying my staff.

My suggestion is to keep it simple for now. With that as a guiding principle, plan to pay your staff wages, staff payroll taxes, and any other staff-related expenses from your Overhead account. Therefore, when you are setting up the accounts, you will need to move the funds from which you withdraw payroll to the Overhead account.

SWITCH THE ACCOUNT FROM WHICH YOU WITHDRAW PAYROLL FUNDS TO THE OVERHEAD ACCOUNT.

Preparing for Payroll

1. Gather time sheets and verify everything is in order.

2. Enter hours in your payroll software (ex: ADP).

3. Add the Owner's Wages and Owner's Payroll Taxes. Move that amount of money from the Owner's Compensation account to the Overhead account.

4. Confirm there is enough money in the Overhead account to cover the entire "cash" required to cover the payroll expenses.

Figure 6.5: Preparing for Payroll

When it's time to run payroll, roughly twice a month, you will need to move money from the Owner's Compensation account to the Overhead account to cover your own salary and payroll wages if you are paid as a W-2 employee. To illustrate: If you are being paid the average wage of $150,000 annually for your work as a dentist, you will need to pay yourself a gross amount of $6,250 every (bimonthly) pay period. You will also need to pay the payroll taxes on that gross amount twice per month. The amount will depend on what your state charges you for payroll taxes and your portion of state unemployment insurance (SUI). Don't worry, you don't have to calculate that number or percentage; you can find it on your payroll report. For the above example, the payroll report (see Figure 6.6) shows the employer portion of taxes to be $475. So you will need to move $6,725 from your Owner's Compensation account over to the Overhead account to fully cover *your* salary. If your children are on your payroll, you will need to do the same thing for their wages on the day you put in the hours to run your payroll. Even if you withdraw money from your "paycheck" to put into your retirement account, that amount is already figured into the gross amount you deposit.

Check Date	Name	Hours	Total Paid	Tax Withheld	Deductions	Net Pay	Ck No	Employer Liability	Total Expense
Pay Frequency: Semimonthly									
5/8/23	Dental Asst.	63.32	2,008.02	392.56	30.12	1,585.34	DD	154.87	2,162.89
5/8/23	Hygienist 1	60.55	2,760.35	587.70	138.01	2,034.64	DD	211.17	2,971.52
5/8/23	Child	20.00	380.00	33.42	0	346.58	DD	33.29	413.29
5/8/23	Hygienist 2	55.93	2,533.48	545.74	0	1,987.74	DD	193.82	2,727.30
5/8/23	Admin Asst.	56.87	1,941.75	385.42	201.75	1,354.58	DD	151.97	2,093.72
5/8/23	Dentist	0	6,725.00	1,691.53	466.53	2,841.94	DD	475.00	5,382.50
Pay Frequency Totals: Semimonthly		**256.67**	**$16,348.60**	**$3,636.37**	**$836.41**	**$10,150.82**		**$1,220.12**	**$17,568.72**
Total Net Pays for Semimonthly frequency: 6									

Figure 6.6: Highlighted Payroll Report

Before you move money from the Owner's Compensation account into the Overhead account, it's a good idea to check and make sure you have enough money in your Overhead account to cover the remainder of the payroll you need to run. If it's tight and/or you don't have enough money in the account to cover it, that should be a sign to you that something must change *immediately*, like a major red flag blowing right into your line of vision. Ideally, if you ran an off-cycle allocation to *all the accounts* from the available income, you would be able to cover your shortfall.

If you do that and still don't have enough money in the Overhead account to cover payroll, you need to double-check right away that all the hours you have entered for each employee are aligned with what each staff member has worked. If something seems off, investigate further to see if you (or they) miscalculated their hours for this payroll period. It could be that someone added hours incorrectly or there was some kind of data entry issue, or perhaps someone set the parameters for the payroll period with the wrong dates.

Payroll *should* be run bimonthly as opposed to every other week. That way, you won't have any months with three pay periods in them and have to worry about additional cash flow management as a result.

PAYROLL PERMISSIONS

I ASKED WILLIAM HILTZ OF Hiltz & Associates, founder of the Dental FraudBusters! Facebook group, to share his thoughts on who should *manage* payroll, and he had the following to say: "Before turning over the editing capabilities of payroll hours to an employee, it's important to have established guidelines and training regarding the employee's responsibilities.

"In terms of recourse, if you observe discrepancies with payroll, it's important to address them promptly. This can involve discussing corrective action with the employee to avoid a future recurrence. If there is evidence of intentional misconduct or negligence, the employee can be disciplined or have their employment terminated, depending on the egregiousness of their negligent or intentional misconduct.

"Most of the payroll fraud occurring in dental practices involves "payroll padding," which is adding bogus time or salary so the employee gets a larger paycheck than they earned. Usually, it is the person who is preparing the payroll. They can bump up their own compensation and have it go unnoticed for long periods of time. That can add up to tens of thousands of dollars.

"Victims of payroll padding are often surprised to learn that their business owner's insurance policy will not cover the loss and that law enforcement is uninterested in arresting or prosecuting the employee. In most cases, it is difficult to prove that the employee did not work the extra time. And because you authorized the employee to process payroll, it can be argued that the employee had your consent to increase their own paycheck and that you failed to perform any oversight of the employee's actions."[34]

WHEN YOU DON'T HAVE ENOUGH MONEY TO COVER PAYROLL

IF YOUR OVERHEAD ACCOUNT CAN'T cover payroll but all seems to be above board and in order, it should be a clear indication that you have not collected enough to cover your payroll expenses. And if your Overhead account was inadequately funded, it means one of three things: one, you didn't collect enough; two, your staff expenses have risen above the ideal percentage range; or three, you spent more than usual on other operating expenses. Diagnosing the issue will involve a deeper discussion, either with someone like me or your accountant, to determine exactly why it has occurred. Obviously, your team must be paid for the time they have already worked. That means you will have to cover their payroll either with an off-cycle distribution of Income funds or a normal allocation before the actual withdrawal for payroll is due.

TAKE A DEEP BREATH

I KNOW THIS CHAPTER IS jam-packed with lots of intimidating tasks. Early in the book, I purposely addressed some of the reasons why you might stop before you ever really get started. This is one of those moments and I wanted you to be prepared.

This book has the tips and tricks to help make this process easier for you. You can reference this chapter at any time as you move forward with implementation. You've got this!

CHAPTER 7
MAXIMIZE EACH DAY

WHEN I WAS IN COLLEGE, I quickly determined that I would not be pursuing architectural engineering as I had originally planned. However, I had no idea what I was going to do with the rest of my life. When I was home over a break, I went in for my dental checkup and cleaning. As always, Dr. Burton chatted with me toward the end of the appointment. He told me that he too had started in engineering before switching over to a predental curriculum. I will never forget him asking me, "Have you ever thought about going into dentistry?" Honestly, I had not.

Dr. Burton could tell I was intrigued and mulling it over, so he added, "Dentistry is a great profession. You make a decent income, set your own schedule, and work as little or as much as you want. You're in charge."

This conversation occurred well before emojis were a thing, but had they been, the little mind-blown face would have been totally appropriate to express how I felt. Since I visited a male dentist and didn't know any female dentists, the job had never come across my radar. As often as my parents told me "You can be anything you want to be," I had never even considered that I, or any female for that matter, could become a dentist. Hindsight always makes it crystal clear to me how little we know when we are fumbling through the decision-making process of "what to be when we grow up."

When I went back to school, I immediately joined the "Predental Society" and toured several dental schools. I changed my major and began investigating entrance requirements for dental schools in the states closest to Kansas. I would indeed pursue a career in dentistry.

Dr. Burton remained our family dentist until my parents moved away from Wichita. At every visit, my mother would give him an update on me. I know she and I both thanked him countless times for suggesting I consider becoming a dentist. I am going to state the obvious here, but please note that Dr. Burton did not emphasize the challenges or tell me how I would have to struggle to get by. He didn't talk about having to cater to patients' demands. He certainly did not mention feeling burned out. He was clearly happy with his choice to become a dentist, so much so that he encouraged me to consider following in his footsteps. I think it was the combination of being able to set my own schedule and being in charge that ultimately sold me on this profession. Every time I have considered changing my office hours or made a tough business decision, I remember that conversation and remind myself that I am indeed in charge. And I do love being involved with health care, even if it means I focus on one small area of the body. I enjoy helping people keep their teeth and maintain their oral health.

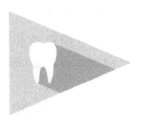

"DENTISTRY IS A GREAT PROFESSION. YOU MAKE A DECENT INCOME, SET YOUR OWN SCHEDULE, AND WORK AS LITTLE OR AS MUCH AS YOU WANT. YOU'RE IN CHARGE."

–DANIEL BURTON, DDS

Earlier, I told you that one of the first things I did as a new practice owner was change our clinical hours of operation. I then changed them yet again a few years later to adapt to my school-age child's schedule. You can do these things as well. That's one of the many benefits of being an owner.

I have said it before, and I plan to keep saying it until you finally believe me: ***You do not have to produce more to make more!*** To make more, you have to *work smarter*. To be more profitable, you must decrease expenses, increase revenue, or do both simultaneously. You must learn to think like a dentist officer in charge!

I have already spent some time discussing ways to cut costs within your practice; now I want to spend time helping you figure out how to *make more*—either for you to take home or to keep within the business—without having to work or produce more.

THE IMPORTANCE OF A SCHEDULE

WE KNOW INTUITIVELY THAT THE way our day goes, and production and collections, will depend on what is scheduled.

However, many dentists don't know how to go about setting up an "ideal day." There are several key principles to keep in mind as you figure out how to tweak the schedule to reach the goals you have for your practice.

As an associate, I worked the hours that my boss dictated. My chairs, or side of the schedule, were planned much like his. At that time, I would see a surgery patient first thing in the morning and then alternate exams and surgeries for the remainder of the day. Our schedule was computerized, but it was still the old DOS style. For those of you who are too young to remember a time before Windows, this meant that our schedule was set up in a non-graphical interface. Patients couldn't "see" openings or the schedule at all, they could only choose the type of appointment they needed and look for available time slots. Or they chose me as the provider and picked "surgery" or "exam" to get a list of available slots. Each appointment block was one hour long. On the hygiene side, we never held back slots for half-mouth scaling and root planing (SRP) appointments, so to fit them in, the scheduling coordinator would simply move other patients to accommodate the SRP patients. I hated the fact that we were moving patient appointment times seemingly at the last minute, and not respecting the fact that the recurring maintenance patients had scheduled those appointments at least three months before, at the end of their previous appointments.

It wasn't until I purchased the practice two years later that we had a system where I could actually see a full day at a time—doctors' and hygiene chairs—and set up blocks of time based on what kind of procedures I wanted to do when. We didn't change much immediately other than hold two-hour blocks on the hygiene side to accommodate the new patients that would need SRP without disrupting the patients who were already scheduled. I still alternated between surgeries and exams. Sometimes that meant my surgeries extended into my exam times because I wasn't as fast as my boss, who had been performing those procedures for roughly thirty years. When I thought something might take me a little longer, I had the scheduling coordinator block out the exam time following the surgery, allowing me a full two hours to get everything done. I didn't give much more thought to it than that. Any kind of surgery could be booked at any of the available times.

Way back then, I didn't have any physical limitations that made it painful by the end of the day if I did four quadrants of osseous regenerative therapy that involve flap reflection, debridement with root planing, osseous contouring with a handpiece, placement of the graft, and membranes and suturing. Now, my wrists, hands, and forearms ache if I do more than two quads of that kind of surgery in one day.

BLOCK SCHEDULING

I WOULDN'T LEARN ABOUT "BLOCK scheduling" for many years, even though I was essentially using a primitive form of it early on. True block scheduling involves planning out blocks of time that help you create an "ideal day" and allow for the best use of your time. If the team schedules accordingly, you should reach your desired production and collections goals and have the right mix of procedures. You basically create a template within your scheduling software that maps out when and where you would like to conduct certain procedures throughout the day. It should be utilized for all the chairs in your practice. Most dental software on the market lets you plan down to ten-minute increments.

To truly maximize block scheduling, you should do a few things: time your procedures, do what's most productive first, and determine what makes an ideal day.

1. **Time Your Procedures** – This is a trick I picked up while working with the Levin Group on implementing better systems. Our consultant told us to start a timer and keep it running for all *active time* patients spent in the chair for a procedure. That includes taking the patient's vital signs, placing topical anesthetic, numbing the patient, the actual procedure, the review of post-op instructions, etc. She then had us try to do each procedure as efficiently as possible, without much downtime for the patient, so that we could get a better sense of how much time we truly needed to allow for each procedure. For instance, in my office, if I have a connective tissue graft planned for teeth #4 and #5, I can easily access the teeth, harvest the graft, and suture everything securely in less than twenty minutes. It might take longer if the patient opts for nitrous oxide, if they ask a lot of questions, or if I get held up in one of the hygienist's rooms discussing recommended treatment with an existing patient and it takes longer than a routine check. I might even take a few minutes to catch up on chart notes or check Facebook at my desk. Even knowing there would be some variation, we could more

accurately plan our day and keep to our schedule by timing
our most common procedures.

TIMED PROCEDURES

PROCEDURE 1:
_____

Asst Time Needed _____

Dr Time Needed _____

Total time _____

AVG TIME TO BLOCK _____

PROCEDURE 2:
_____

Asst Time Needed _____

Dr Time Needed _____

Total time _____

AVG TIME TO BLOCK _____

PROCEDURE 3:
_____

Asst Time Needed _____

Dr Time Needed _____

Total time _____

AVG TIME TO BLOCK _____

Figure 7.1: Common Procedures and Time Needed

2. **Do What's Most Productive First** – I mean literally, first thing. In my practice, that means I get to pick up my #15 blades and start cutting first thing. I no longer alternate between surgical procedures and exams. I focus on surgeries and perform them before lunch. I was reluctant to implement this and openly admitted to the consultant that I'm not a morning person. She reasoned that if I knocked the surgeries out first thing, our biggest production would all be done before noon. That meant that if I wasn't feeling well, or received a phone call from my daughter's school and had to leave to pick her up, we would still have a decent chance of reaching our production and collections goals for the day. Additionally, if a new patient didn't show up for an evaluation toward the end of the day, we could potentially leave earlier rather than have to find other tasks to do to keep busy. I gave it a try and have never looked back.

3. **Determine What Makes an Ideal Day** – This is slightly more complicated than it sounds. The first thing I want you to do is find your best *and* worst months within the past twelve months in terms of production. Evaluate the months as a whole and record how many of your top ten procedures were done in both the best and worst production months. What are the major discrepancies? Were you out with COVID-19 during the worst month, or have way more no-shows or cancellations because your patients had the flu? Perhaps tooth extractions took up lots of chair time. On the flip side, maybe during your

most productive month you saw several new patients who all needed crowns and had tax return money burning a hole in their pocket. In my practice, my best months probably include lots of connective tissue grafts, implants, and osseous surgeries, and significantly fewer surgical extractions and frenectomies. Figure out what made your good month so great, and then find the most productive day and see what made it stand out amongst the others. That will give you a great starting point for setting up your ideal block schedule. If you're a periodontist, did you do only surgeries, while your hygienists only saw scaling and root planing patients? Maybe you had a big implant case with multiple extractions, implants, and abutment placement with a temporary denture conversion. Now find the least productive day of your worst month and figure out what made production so low. Did you have to leave early to pick up a sick child? Were there late cancellations that couldn't be filled? Did you open a surgical site, thinking you would be able to do bone grafting around a tooth, only to find a vertical fracture? By looking at the two extremes, you should begin to notice what leads to a higher-production day versus a lower-production day.

While high-production days feel good when they result in a higher amount of revenue coming into the practice, they may not be truly *ideal*. Did that high-production day feel hectic? Were you running behind all day? Did you have to take care of high-maintenance patients? Perhaps you had to do a crown prep on an upper second molar where access was difficult at best. That's all to say that there are other things to consider besides production and collections when setting up your schedule to ideally suit the way you *want* to practice. Do you have any physical limitations that might keep you from setting up a recurring schedule of those super productive days? Can you realistically take back-to-back sedation patients? Are you filling your days with the procedures you not only like to do but are also good at?

You should keep in mind the Pareto principle, also commonly known as the "80/20 rule." In the simplest terms, it states that 80% of your revenue is derived from 20% of your offerings or services. That means you no longer have to do procedures that you dislike. If performing a root canal makes you break into a sweat—as it did me in dental school—refer those patients to an endodontist. Figure out what you *enjoy* doing the most. Then do more of that. Additionally, figure out which patients are your favorites to work on and systematically work to get more of them. For more information on exactly how to go about that, I will refer you to another Mike Michalowicz book, *The Pumpkin Plan*.[35]

As you set up your block scheduling template, don't forget to set aside time to work *on* the practice. Schedule time for team building and to work with your team on carrying out the vision of your practice through the systems you have created. Finally, make sure you have scheduled time to be out of the practice completely—not only for continuing dental education, but also to spend time with your friends or family, either at home or on vacation. You will be happier, healthier, and more productive if you step away every so often.

The quickest way to burn out early and/or often is to think that the practice cannot handle a few days without you. Teach your team how to do things without you and take time off.

REGULARLY REEVALUATE YOUR SCHEDULE

Writing this book took me close to two years. During that time, I began working with Leigh Ann Faight and Tiffany Esterline of Upstream Dental Coaching. I knew I needed help taking my practice to the next level and I felt stuck with a team that was resigned to doing things as they always had. My employees weren't on board with my plan to transition to a fee-for-service practice. I had seen enough friends go through the process of becoming independent providers for insurance to know that consistently providing excellent patient experiences would be necessary. I wanted an outside set of eyes on our team and practice to help us successfully make this change without having to reinvent the wheel.

One step in my fee-for-service journey was reevaluating my schedule—again. Leigh Ann helped me by asking me to find a couple of really "good" days, not just in terms of production but also in terms of the actual patients, patient flow, and procedures performed. She asked me to do the same for a few "bad" days. She then asked a very important question: "What about the good days did you *enjoy*? Why were they such good days?" It turns out I really like the days when I have several surgical procedures and fewer exams. Not only because they are higher-production days, but because I am getting to do what I love. Surgery. I told both Leigh Ann and Tiffany, "I'm always happiest when I'm cutting." That is part of why the days when I did tons of new patient exams were mentally exhausting for me.

They suggested moving new patient exam blocks to the hygiene schedule so that the hygienists could do most of the information-gathering for me *and* begin establishing a relationship with those patients. My mind was blown. I had never even considered that a possibility, even though I knew most general dentists handle new patients that way.

Once I agreed to give it try, Tiffany analyzed my patient software numbers to help me figure out how many blocks of time we needed for surgeries, new patient exams, scaling and root planing appointments, post-op appointments, and checkups. She then drafted a block schedule for us to review and the provide feedback. One critical part of Upstream's coaching philosophy, and one step most owners want to skip, is time for the team to weigh in on any proposed change. Before we implemented the schedule changes, we spent time reviewing the new layout together.

Initially, we had most of the 7:30 a.m. hygiene appointments blocked for scaling and root planing or new patient exams.

The hygienists let Tiffany know that many of our long-term periodontal maintenance patients liked those 7:30 a.m. appointments, so we adjusted accordingly. We also spelled out the specifics of what kinds of surgeries should be done each day. Creating enough variation in the schedule ensured that I wasn't sore from full days of performing bone grafting procedures on patients with severe disease.

Some of my long-term staff wasn't so sure about it at first, so Tiffany suggested we start with one new "ideal" day per week. However, my new hygienists were totally on board since they would get a physical break from seeing patients for periodontal maintenance and scaling and root planing appointments. Therefore, we began implementing close to the new ideal schedule right away.

To keep this schedule in motion, about a month in advance I must go in and tweak a few things based on my time out of the office, which limits when and where hygienists can see new patients and perform scaling and root planing. We do try to make sure we purposely book periodontal maintenance patients that have recently had a periodic exam during weeks when I am out of the office.

Switching to this block schedule has also made it easier to work without having a dedicated surgical assistant. One of my former surgical assistants has transitioned to the financial coordinator position and we have been unable to find an adequate replacement. We no longer need a full-time surgical assistant on our ideal days, as the hygienists are doing more in terms of sterilization, postoperative management, and new patient exams.

At a time when finding good employees was difficult, we successfully implemented a workaround that not only helped keep employee costs down, but also allowed us to practice in a manner that suits our needs and deliver more personalized care to each patient without me having to rush from room to room all day long.

THE IMPORTANCE OF SYSTEMS

YOU DON'T HAVE TO BROWSE in the business section of a bookstore very long before you realize that having systems in place is probably a good idea. Two of the books I love on this topic are *The Checklist Manifesto*[36] and *The E-Myth Dentist.*[37] Even before I read those books, I knew the importance of having well-trained staff members who are also cross-trained as much as possible. Unfortunately, this was another lesson I had to learn the hard way.

When I originally took over the reins of my periodontal practice, I hired all but one of the hygienists. What I wasn't expecting was for the front desk person/scheduling coordinator to come in after the first pay period and tell me that the previous owner had promised her a raise if she stayed. I was furious. She wasn't his employee anymore and he had no right to make that promise. Since he was still working as my associate at that point, I asked him about it. He told me that he had been scared she would leave. Unfortunately, I was not confident enough as a new owner to remind her that her pay was determined by me, not him. She continued to work there, but I immediately learned all the other aspects of the nonclinical team. I had my mother come in and learn how to schedule patients, take payments, and do all the other miscellaneous administrative duties. I figured that this way, even if someone was sick, my mom could fill in. If the worst-case scenario happened and one of the nonclinical team members quit, my mom could fill in and help train a new person so that I could continue to focus on the periodontal side of the practice.

Having been in private practice for close to two decades, I have seen and trained numerous team members. We have radically changed many things about our practice, including converting from an archaic DOS scheduling system to our current software, switching from old-school radiographs and developing films in a darkroom to digital radiography, and no longer using paper charts or dictating treatment notes. Our procedure manual has been rewritten and updated numerous times and will always be a work in progress.

Systems allow you to maximize your team members' strengths and compensate for when you're down a member or two. This is imperative for your success. As so eloquently stated in *The E-Myth Dentist*, systems are what allow the owner's vision to be "consistently and faithfully manifested at the operating level of the business."[38]

DON'T OVERSELL — BUT DON'T HOLD YOURSELF BACK

WHEN I FIRST MET WITH Dr. Yelena Shirkin and Dr. Rebecca Allen of Baltimore Dental at the end of 2021, I was impressed with how much of the practice collections were going to the two partners. Their reported collection revenue was up more than 10% that year, which was definitely not the norm for our industry unless someone had inadvertently applied grant funds to revenue, so I double-checked that with them. They confirmed that the collection revenue only included income related to providing dentistry in their offices. I then inquired if they were a fee-for-service practice, as most practices that participated in insurance were not doing as well as they were. They both smiled and Rebecca said, "No, we even participate with some PPOs."

After giving them generous praise for the success they were already having, I asked if they would tell me what they had done differently in 2021 that led to their growth. They told me about four changes they had made. First, they got Bioclear-certified and offered that restorative option to their patients. Second, they implemented a bonus system for the entire office based on collections per day. Third, they implemented a hygienist bonus system based on fluoride application and sealants done on maintenance patients. And last, they offered an in-house payment plan. I was unfamiliar with Bioclear and asked if it was yet another company involved with clear aligner technology. They politely explained that it was a restorative option using moldable composites, making it an affordable option for patients that didn't want or need full coverage crowns. They had spent the time and money necessary to learn the new skills, and their whole team was excited about being able to offer better restorative options for bread-and-butter dentistry.

As I finished writing this book, I asked Yelena and Rebecca if I could share some of their stories with you. They generously shared the changes they had decided to implement since we originally met in 2021. During 2022, they had successfully introduced Invisalign to their practice, and that meant they were now offering clear aligner teeth straightening. I made sure they had double-checked that their expenses hadn't increased by the same amount as their collections, as I have seen many times when practices first begin aligner therapy. Yelena told me she had figured out early on that they needed to separate the lab cost of each new case and hold it in a separate bank account before allocating any funds to their traditional Profit First accounts. I practically jumped up and down with excitement—they had used cash management to avoid lab bill surprises! The past year they had bonused individual team members for "closing" new aligner cases. This year, they planned to apply $100 per new Invisalign case toward a team bonus to help them get to the next level of Invisalign provider so that their per-case lab fees would be further reduced. They also planned to keep doing the hygiene bonus of $5 per sealant and $3 per fluoride application for existing maintenance patients and merely tweak the team bonus parameters so it was based on an annual rather than daily goal. When I asked if they were able to keep up the pace of this high-production practice, and if they wanted to continue as is, they told me that next up was to start eliminating their lowest-paying insurance plans so they could work smarter rather than harder. I was glad to see that they were continuing to reevaluate if they were practicing the way they wanted to and adjusting as necessary to meet their changing wants and needs.

SMALL CHANGES LEAD TO BIG GAINS

NOTHING CHANGES WITHOUT EFFORT, BUT you don't have to go big or go home. The dentists of Baltimore Dental are living proof that you don't even have to operate as fee-for-service to take home what you deserve. Implementing systems and making seemingly insignificant changes can lead to major shifts for you, your collections, your team dynamics, and even your mental health. Bravo for making it farther up Profit Mountain!

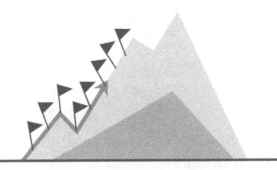

CHAPTER 8
GET PAID FOR WHAT YOU DO

IT SEEMS SIMPLE ENOUGH THAT we should get paid for services we provide at the time we provide them. However, we all know that is often not the case. Patients are used to being billed for healthcare services once their insurance coverage has been paid. Many times, they are surprised that we expect an estimated co-pay, or even the full fee, on the day services are provided. I am embarrassed to recall how many times I've heard my residency director's voice in my head, saying, "When you go to the grocery store to buy a gallon of milk, do you get to leave without paying?" I used to be so annoyed when he made us postpone surgical cases if patients didn't arrive with the money needed to pay for their procedures. Yet he had a valid point. We should expect payment. We are providing a service and to do that, we incur expenses.

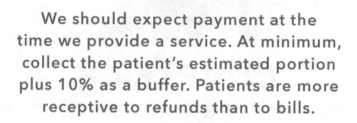

> We should expect payment at the time we provide a service. At minimum, collect the patient's estimated portion plus 10% as a buffer. Patients are more receptive to refunds than to bills.

Being clear with your team and patients about when and how you expect to receive payments is one of the first skills you must master to stay in business. You should have clearly stated financial policies on your website and on your new-patient paperwork. After reviewing treatment plans with your patient, someone from your team should give them information about their financial obligations, including what the cost of services will be if insurance doesn't pay for anything. Your diagnosis and treatment options *should not* be based on what you think the patient's financial situation is or what they're willing to pay. You might be surprised by what people will pay for when you present the facts. I know that was certainly the case for me and my team when we learned better ways to present full arch restorative options, ranging from a traditional denture up to the implant-supported fixed appliance.

Your diagnosis and recommended treatment *should not*—I repeat, *not*—be based on what the patient's insurance might cover or whether they have used all their benefits for the year. We all know that insurance maximums and reimbursements have not changed much in the past fifty years, while dental technology and expertise have grown exponentially. Insurance companies have a way of blaming these decisions on the employers who choose certain plans; however, the insurance companies are the ones that present the various plans to the companies that choose them. Insurance companies are concerned about their bottom line. One of the clearest examples of this archaic thinking is that topical fluoride varnish is rarely a covered benefit for adults. However, patients can have recurrent decay around existing fillings or crowns. Many adults develop new carious lesions on exposed root surfaces. To fix those cavities will cost the patients time and money. It will also cost insurance companies money. Wouldn't it make more sense to cover preventative treatment? Wouldn't that be better for both parties? How about the employers who must allow their employees time off to visit the dentist? For as much bad press as the Veteran's Administration (VA) has received over the past several years, I find it worth noting that the VA covers topical fluoride for adults and pays better for many of the surgical services I provide.

PROPER CODING

ONCE YOU HAVE EVALUATED YOUR patient, made a diagnosis, and formulated a treatment plan, you need to know how to properly code for the various procedures necessary to accomplish the goal of returning your patient to health, or at least halting disease progression. You must also understand what is included when you bill out for certain things. For instance, when I perform a connective tissue graft, I cannot bill out separately for anesthetic or suture removal like I could if I were a physician or nurse. Those things are considered included in the content of service.

Eighteen years into practice, I learned that I could have billed out for subgingival irrigation and been reimbursed by *most* insurance companies. I could also charge for a full periodontal comprehensive evaluation (D0180) once per year if I saw the patient and we collected and charted all the information included as part of that examination. Legally, I have to see patients once per year, and we definitely collect all that information, but unfortunately, I did not know how to properly bill for the services we provided. Ironically, I learned this particular pearl at a workshop I co-led with Dr. Stephanie Mapp of Mapp Your Practice.[39]

There are courses available to teach you or your administrative team about proper insurance coding. I know that both the American Academy of Periodontology (AAP) and the American Dental Association (ADA) offer some. A quick call or email to your dental societies, or even asking colleagues on social media, should make it relatively easy to find a course on proper coding that is suited to your practice.

CLAIMS SUBMISSION

IDEALLY YOU WILL HAVE EITHER collected money from the patient for all the services provided on the same day or, at minimum, what you expect them to owe once insurance has been processed. Unless you are a fee-for-service practice that doesn't file claims for your payments, it's imperative that you submit the claims each day once you have completed the dentistry and appropriately coded all your work. Each dental software has different protocols for submitting electronic claims, but I suggest you submit electronically as much as possible. Many times, you will have to add additional software and/or systems to attach photos, chart notes, and radiographs to claims for your bigger procedures.

Don't forget, some insurance companies will require more information than others to process your claim on the first pass. The perfect example of that in my situation is when I submit a claim for connective tissue grafting to Delta Dental. They are the only insurance company I am aware of that requires me to submit a periapical (PA) radiograph of the tooth or teeth involved in this soft tissue procedure. You can avoid headaches, additional work for your nonclinical team, and delays by learning these nuances.

ACCOUNTS RECEIVABLE FOLLOW-THROUGH

AN IMPORTANT PIECE OF CASH flow management that is often overlooked is accounts receivable, the outstanding balances on your patient accounts for services already provided. The further out you go from the date of services, the less likely you are to get paid. The rule of thumb is to have less than 5% of your accounts receivable in the more-than-ninety-days category. I admit, this is something I didn't pay close enough attention to until much later in my career. I just assumed we were keeping up on unpaid claims and overdue balances—and you know what they say about assuming anything.

I pull the unpaid claims report, aging report, and credit balance report bimonthly, at least; ideally, I review them once per week and then pass them on to my administrative team.

1. **Unpaid Claims Report** – Within my patient software, I set the report parameters for one year before the date I run the report through thirty days before that date. For example, if today is April 30, 2023, I will pull up the unpaid claims report for April 1, 2022, through March 31, 2023. This report shows the insurance company, patient name, date of service, original date the claim was sent, whether it was sent electronically or by mail, and the date of the most recent resubmission, if applicable. It also shows the amount submitted on the claim and the patient balance. I compare the report to the one I ran previously and then prioritize which claims I would like one of my nonclinical team members to follow up on. Sometimes I want them to resubmit, especially for something like periodontal maintenance services. Other times, I have them reach out via email to one of our insurance representatives.

   Lastly, I have them call the insurance companies directly to follow up on these claims. I emphasize that this is the last resort because it can tie up a phone line and a significant portion of that employee's time. If we continue to have issues with nonpayment, I file an online complaint with our state insurance commissioner and they will launch an investigation into the claim for the patient. Unfortunately, there is little they can do about claims submitted to insurance companies out of state.

2. **Aging Report** – Our aging report lists all the patients with outstanding balances and breaks those balances into categories: those that are considered current (30 days or less), 31–60 days past the date of service, 61–90 days past the date of service, 91–120 days past the date of service, and 121 days or more past the date of service. Ideally, 90% of these outstanding balances should be under 61 days, an indication that you have received both the insurance payments and the patients' expected portions of those payments promptly. We all know that insurance companies often take longer than 30 days to process claims; patients with dual insurance coverage will take even longer to be processed. I review this report to see what percentage is under 61 days and what is over 90 days to check the pulse of how well we are following up on our receivables.

	Current	31–60 days	61–90 days	91+ days
Balance				

Figure 8.1 Accounts Receivable Breakdown

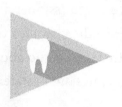

YOU WANT TO KEEP THE OVER 90 DAYS ACCOUNTS RECEIVABLE (AR) TO 5% OR LESS OF THE TOTAL OUTSTANDING AR.

I also have one of my nonclinical team members do a deep dive into those balances that are 91 days or more past the date of service. They compare those names to those on the unpaid claims report and follow up accordingly, calling patients to explain that we have not received payment from their insurance company within 90 days and therefore, the patients are responsible for the full payment for services provided and can call the insurance company to try to assist in the process. If insurance has already been paid and the patient has an outstanding balance they aren't paying, we make a phone call to try to take care of payment over the phone. If we get no response to that phone call, which we will have documented, we send them a written warning that if payment is not received within fifteen days of the date on the warning letter, their future appointments will be canceled and their balance turned over to a collection agency.

I know that many dentists are reluctant to turn patients over to collections, but I do not hesitate to do so if the patient is not taking an active role in paying off the balance for services already provided. I have always used a law firm that specializes in collections for this aspect of my practice and haven't pursued filing anything in small claims court myself, as I know I can make better use of my time doing something else.

3. **Credit Balance Report** – While this report shows you which accounts have a credit on their account—in other words, you owe them money—it's still an important report to review in terms of cash flow. Before any action is taken to refund money to the patient, I personally review each account to make sure that the entries are accurate. Since I was recently in-network with a couple of insurance companies, that means I need to pull the estimate of benefits (EOB) and confirm that any payments and write-offs are accurate. If all that appears in order, we call the patient and ask if they would like us to refund them the credit or keep it on the account.

I issue refunds using the same form of payment the patient did. In other words, if the patient paid with a credit card, I refund to their credit card. If they wrote a check, I cut them a check through the bill-pay feature of my Overhead account. When I spoke with William Hiltz of Hiltz & Associates, founder of the Dental FraudBusters! Facebook group, he said: "Unless there is a compelling reason to do otherwise, refunds should be issued by check. Patient refunds should not be issued to a credit or debit card without proper authorization. Use the settings of your merchant terminal to restrict access to credit and debit card refunds. This will prevent an employee or anyone else from using your merchant terminal to issue refunds without proper authorization (i.e., an "override"). When a credit card refund is required, it should only be issued to the same, previously used credit card, and require your override. Practice owners can contact their merchant service company to learn more or to request assistance with these features.

"When issuing a check refund, do not write a check and hand it to an employee to put in the mail. To ensure that the check reaches its intended destination, ask your employee to provide you with a stamped envelope with the patient's address on it so you can mail it yourself. In the envelope, your employee should include a refund letter addressed to the patient explaining why the refund was issued and a copy of the patient's account statement that shows the refund."[40]

You can download sample patient refund letters at dentalfraudbusters.com/issuing-refunds-in-your-dental-practice/.

YOU ARE THE ONLY PERSON IN YOUR PRACTICE WHO SHOULD BE AUTHORIZED TO ISSUE REFUNDS, NO MATTER THE TENDER.

We can make a note in our software if a patient would like us to keep the credit on their account until their next appointment. If there is no such note, we call the patient and see what they would like us to do. The one exception to that is if the patient has Blue Cross Blue Shield as their insurance provider. Blue Cross Blue Shield requires us to return an overpayment to the patient rather than keeping the credit on their account.

There are times when patients do not have future appointments in our office, such as when they come in for one area of connective tissue grafting. When that is the case, we try to return the credit balance as quickly as possible. If the patient paid with a debit or credit card, I process the return to their credit card without needing to speak to them about it and simply send them a copy of the receipt. I issue a refund check if they paid with cash or wrote us a personal check. If the check remains uncashed, I must report the balance to the unclaimed property department of the State of Kansas. At that time, I make a note on their transaction screen that they never cashed the refund check. That way, if they return for any services in the future, we can apply the credit toward the new charges.

ACCEPTED FORMS OF PAYMENT

UP UNTIL THIS POINT IN the chapter, I have mainly discussed how to get paid for what you do after it has been done. However, the best way to get paid is on the day the services are provided or even before. Many practice owners I know require patients to pay some or all of the fee before the day of service to minimize late cancellations and make sure they get paid. At my office, for surgical patients, we collect (at least) the expected patient portion of the fee for services provided before the patient goes back to the surgical operatory. We give a discount to those paying over a certain amount. The size of the discount is based on what form of payment they use—cash, check, or credit card. If they pay via a third-party billing company like Care Credit, we do not offer a discount.

LOSE THE GUILT

THERE ARE OTHER WAYS TO get paid or increase cash flow, such as offering in-house membership plans or requiring scheduling deposits that I will only mention here as they are highly specific to each practice. The main takeaway of this chapter should be that you make sure your patients have options to pay for the services you provide so that they can address their treatment needs *and* you can earn a living. No one working in your office should feel guilty for expecting patients to pay for their services. We all must pay for the goods and services we receive. Plus, patients take our cues from us, so we should *value* the care we provide to them.

As it gets easier and easier to ask for *and* receive the money you deserve for providing patient care, your focus will likely switch over to questions about which debts you should try to tackle, or how to decide how much cash to keep on hand now that there is an excess. We will review all of that in the next chapter. For now, enjoy breathing a little easier on your path up Profit Mountain.

CHAPTER 9
DEAL WITH DEBT

MY SINGLE-MINDED FOCUS BACK IN the mid-1990s was on doing whatever it took to be a strong candidate for dental school admissions. I participated in the appropriate social and volunteer activities, made sure I kept up my grade point average, and prepared for the dreaded Dental Admission Test (DAT®). Even when I headed off to my interview in my hot pink suit, pantyhose, and heels, I was still completely clueless about the cost of dental school. Maybe it was the permed big hair that obscured that detail from my vision. All I know is that I was blissfully unaware of the cost of dental education.

Don't get me wrong, I was not born with a silver spoon in my mouth. Quite the opposite. I arrived a month early and spent my first few days sleeping in a drawer of one of the chests at my parents' "fancy" student housing at the University of Texas—a trailer in the married student housing section (in the early 1970s, trailers were considered a step up from the old World War II barracks that had been converted into living quarters).

Our living situation certainly improved once my dad finished his PhD in aerospace engineering and my mom completed her undergraduate degree in education. I was well cared for. We always had a home and I felt safe and loved. I did not even know food insecurity was an actual problem until I became a parent myself and got involved with my daughter's school. While I had it better than many of my peers, I was by no means a trust fund kid with unlimited means to attend college. I was simply ignorant.

I did know I could apply for government loans, which had low-interest rates at the time. If I was accepted to the University of Missouri-Kansas City School of Dentistry, I would receive in-state tuition rates; the state of Kansas had secured a handful of seats in each dental class there since there is no specialized dental school in Kansas. My parents had told me they were willing to help cover my living expenses, but all the tuition and school supply expenses would be mine. By the time I started looking into periodontal residencies, I thought I understood the costs slightly better. However, my dad still wonders why I didn't choose the residency that paid a small percentage of the revenue collected for the services I provided.

While at Baylor for my periodontal residency, I received a scholarship that covered my tuition and supply expenses. I used student loans for those three years so I could cover most of my living expenses. As strange as it sounds to me now, I never worried or even thought much about the repayment of those loans. I had complete confidence in my ability to become a periodontist and have a successful career. I wouldn't feel the weight of that financial burden for a dozen years post-residency.

By then, it felt as if I was pinned under a very well-fed, male African elephant. You know, the big ones that weigh up to 14,000 pounds!

When I was doing my exit interview at Baylor and speaking with the school counselor about consolidating my loans, I asked her a very morbid question about what would happen to my loans if something happened to me. Unfortunately, the question was all too pertinent for our family, as my sister's husband's undergraduate loans were forgiven upon his death. The financial aid counselor told me to check the fine print of any consolidation paperwork, but that most loans had provisions for times of financial or physical hardship, and most had a death clause. I was able to consolidate my loans for an interest rate of 3.25% over thirty years, and my loan would indeed be forgiven should I die before it was paid off. Due to the low-interest rate, "reasonable" monthly payment amount, and the fact that it would not affect my estate should I die, it was not a priority for me to pay it off early.

I expect you have probably completed dental school, or are at least currently enrolled, and have already accumulated student loan debt. Since repayment might be a concern, I want to address it here. I know that interest rates and the cost of tuition are significantly higher for newer graduates. Therefore, your decisions about whether to pay extra on student loan(s) and whether to consider more debt to purchase a practice or do a start-up are much more complicated than they were for me. "Which debt should be taken care of first?" is an all-too-common question asked by my colleagues. There is no perfect answer, and it will always be a very personal choice for you, but I will review some of the points to evaluate while making that decision.

So, let's talk about the ever-present elephant in the room—debt. All the debt, not just education-related but also practice-related. Let's talk about how to be smart about taking on new debt, options for paying it off, various strategies to do so, and how debt affects your cash flow. I want to make sure you're not crushed by the weight of that well-fed African elephant.

ALL DEBT MATTERS

THERE ARE A FEW STUDENTS who have little to no debt because they had financial support from their families, worked numerous jobs while attending both undergraduate and professional programs, received scholarships, participated in the Health Professions Scholarship Program (HPSP) through one of the branches of the U.S. military, or some combination of the above. I surveyed more than three hundred dentists who graduated within the last twenty-five years, and their responses indicated that the most common amount of debt incurred is somewhere between $200,000 and $250,000. Some reported spending over half a million dollars to earn their dental degree and cover their living expenses.

In addition to education-related debt, there are also concerns about personal and business debt for those who own practices. Of course, these are all intricately linked. At a Collier, Sarner & Associates seminar I attended in Orlando in the early 2000s, the speaker told the room, "The best piece of financial advice I can give you is to choose your spouse wisely."[41] This got some chuckles from the crowd, but he went on to describe several instances in which bad marriages caused catastrophic damage to dentists' financial health.

At the time, I remember thinking, *Well, this advice would have been more helpful to the attendees before we even became dentists.* You may be thinking the same thing as you read this. As it turns out, his words would come back to haunt me when I divorced my daughter's father several years later. While I did lose a significant amount of money in the divorce, my earnings as a dentist gave me the financial flexibility to recover.

To further illustrate the point that all finances are personal, let's consider "Dr. Walker's" path to practice ownership. After finishing up a pediatric residency, he moved back to his home state of Colorado where his fiancée, a woman he had dated during dental school, lived. She worked all through dental school as an elementary school teacher and had well-established connections, a steady paycheck, and a home he would move into. He was from the area, so it made perfect sense to move back there to establish a practice. He planned to find a good associate position so he could work for a couple of years, save up enough money to qualify for a practice loan, and then make sure the practice he was working in would be his forever dental home.

Everything went great the first couple of years. He got married and worked as an associate at a pediatric practice. While his wife's house was small, it was convenient for their jobs and they only had a dog to worry about. Soon, it was time to secure financing and purchase the practice where he worked. He considered it his dream job. Also, he and his wife were excited to welcome their first baby.

While she focused on the pregnancy and teaching, he began to search for a larger home in the "right" school district. He also began speaking with bankers about loan terms and requirements to proceed with purchasing the practice. He chose to work with a local bank and felt comfortable with the commercial lender he would be dealing with. He gathered up the business financials, his own credit card and bank statements, and his student loan paperwork. Since he and his wife had married well after they were already established as young adults, they had never combined their finances. Therefore, his banker asked him to gather all her information as well.

When she first delayed getting him the information, Dr. Walker was only mildly annoyed. It was the end of the school year and her schedule was full of extra activities. When school was out, he brought it up again and told her that if she pulled her statements, he would get them uploaded to the bank portal.

Dr. Walker was not expecting the tears that began cascading down her cheeks. He couldn't understand why she was crying and practically hyperventilating. He told me about the unease he immediately felt in his stomach. Once she finally caught her breath, his wife admitted to him that she was frightened to turn over the statements. She was worried the bank wouldn't preapprove them for anything.

Still crying, she blurted, "I have a gambling problem. I have three credit cards that I only pay the minimum balance on. When I run out of credit on one, I open a new one."

To say he was flabbergasted would be an understatement. While he grew tenser and his stomach more uneasy, he tried to wrap his head around what his wife had just said. He told me it was as if he was having an out-of-body experience, like it was a scene in a movie he was watching and not his actual life.

"What do you mean you have a gambling problem? What on earth are you betting on? When does a pregnant elementary school teacher have time to gamble? How bad is it? Are you in danger? Do I need to worry that some thug is going to show up here with a baseball bat?"

"No, no, no. We are not in any danger. I don't really know how bad it is since I only focus on paying the minimum amount on my credit cards. I place bets on sports games. It started back in college when I was on the volleyball team," she confessed. "Guys from the football team would get together with some of us to watch the big games on TV. One of the guys always had a hustle going. I got addicted then because it was a lot of fun, and it was easy money. The money I made off those games meant I didn't need a part-time job. Like most of my friends, I gave it up once we left college. When I got in that car accident during my first year of teaching, not only did I have to take time off from work, some of it unpaid, but I also needed to buy a new car. That didn't leave much money in the bank. To top it off, I was depressed after lying around at home every day for six weeks. I stumbled across an online gambling site, and I was hooked again."

To make this long story shorter, I will tell you that Dr. Walker and his wife got counseling— not only to help with the breach of trust but also to figure out how to best manage his wife's addiction and financial woes. Ultimately, they were advised that she should declare bankruptcy, which would allow them to keep their home and make a semi-fresh start. Dr. Walker, his wife, and their attorney had to have a tough conversation with the commercial lender about whether he would even qualify for a business loan. Ultimately, he would indeed get financing, but the bank insisted on proceeding with a Small Business Association (SBA) loan to minimize their risk.

DEBT STRATEGIES

DENTISTS OFTEN FORGET TO CONSIDER debt, and the actual cash needed to make monthly payments, as part of their business overhead. My theory is this is because the principal portion of the debt payments is not recorded on profit and loss statements. The payments must still be made, whether they count as a business expense for tax purposes or not, so that means you must have the cash available to do so. As you begin to manage your cash better by utilizing the Profit First Pearls presented earlier in this book, you will begin to have more profit. Once you have more profit, you have more options—so should you pay down your debt? Should you take more money home? Should you pay down your student loans, mortgage, or business debt?

At this point, I must remind you that I am *not* a certified financial advisor. And I recommend that you discuss these options with your accountant and/or financial advisor. I will review a few basics on the various debt strategies so you are better prepared for the meeting you will have with them to choose what's best for you and your circumstances. As you prepare for that meeting, I do think it would be helpful to have every single debtor listed, with the current interest rate, the total amount owed, and the amount of each monthly payment. You should gather this information for the current and long-term liabilities of the business, your personal debts, including student loans, mortgages, car loans, etc., and any other IOUs that involve money owed to a third party. That information will be necessary to help you choose how to tackle your debt.

TOTAL DEBTS			
Creditor	Balance	Interest Rate	Min Mthly Payment
1			
2			
3			
4			
5			

Figure 9.1: Debt Worksheet

For any of the following plans to work, and for you to have the momentum to keep them going, you must implement a "debt freeze," which means you will no longer purchase things you cannot pay for immediately. If that means you cut up your credit cards and only initiate checks from the bill-pay feature, then do that. If you have to give up traveling to your favorite CE event for a year and find courses closer to home or free classes online, do that. Otherwise, it will be like you are trying to keep cool in your Southern home by wearing the least amount of clothing as is socially acceptable, running the air conditioning, and sipping iced tea—sweet, of course—while the other occupants of your house have windows open on the second floor and multiple loads of clothes cycling through the dryer while baking lasagna in the preheated oven. Though your efforts may help make you feel marginally cooler, they may not even make a noticeable difference.

If you're like me, you may feel frustrated and defeated when facing down debt—and that is definitely *not* how I want you to feel when you are tackling any kind of money issue. I want you to feel confident and capable. I want your goals to feel attainable. If they don't, you will likely not only give up but also sink further into financial trouble. Once you get your debt freeze going, I want you to figure out which of the following strategies makes the most sense for you.

The three main debt strategies are "debt snowball," "debt avalanche," and "debt consolidation."

1. **Debt Snowball**[42] - This strategy involves making the minimum payment on all the debts listed. *Extra cash is then applied to the debt with the smallest outstanding balance.* Not the one with the highest interest rate or the one with the shortest time remaining until payoff, but the one with the smallest outstanding balance. This continues until that debt is paid off, and then the minimum monthly payment that used to go toward that debt is lumped into the extra cash to pay off the debt with the next smallest outstanding

balance. As more debt is paid off, the amount of cash available to apply to the next debt gets larger and larger, like a snowball rolling down the mountain. The pro of this method is that it gets you an early win.

2. **Debt Avalanche** – With this strategy, once the minimum payments are made on all debts, *extra cash is funneled to the debt with the highest interest rate.* No consideration is given to how much is owed on that debt, how long it might take to pay it off before you tackle the next one, or the size of the monthly payment. While it certainly addresses the issue of your increased debt due to the higher interest rate on the outstanding balance, it could take a long time to feel a sense of accomplishment and like you are decreasing the size of that African elephant on your shoulders. On the other hand, once that debt is paid off, it *might* feel like a bigger win.

3. **Debt Consolidation** – This strategy consists of several components, including combining the outstanding balance of loans and credit cards to pay fewer debtors, with the hopes of refinancing for lower interest rates and lower monthly payments. Sometimes the lower payments come at the cost of a longer payoff term; however, if there is no prepayment penalty, you can still employ one of the two strategies above to pay down the debt more quickly when money is not so tight.

Often, when I conduct Limited Financial Exams for dentists, I come across six or seven different notes they're paying on every single month. Sometimes the owners have no idea what the monthly payment or the interest rate on the loan is, or even how long it will take until the debt is paid off. One dentist accidentally paid several additional months on a loan after it was paid off. Thankfully, her overpayments were returned to her promptly. This happens more often than you might think with automated payments. If someone is having cash flow problems to the point where they're struggling to cover payroll or pay their credit card bills each month, one of the things I evaluate is the terms of their existing debt. Could they free up more cash in the business right away by consolidating and/or refinancing? This is another time when having an existing relationship with a banker can be quite beneficial. (Certainly, prepayment penalties must be evaluated closely.)

DON'T WAIT TO TAKE YOUR PROFIT FIRST

IF YOU ARE BEING CRUSHED by that giant elephant, do not delay implementing Profit First. You might tell me it doesn't make sense to make a profit if you still have debt, but I am living proof that you will proceed up Profit Mountain much more quickly and with way less fatigue if you *use your profit to get the elephant off your back.* Debt can be physically, mentally, emotionally, *and* financially crushing.

When you're thinking about why you should proceed with Profit First even though you have debt, there are two main points to remember. First, it's a cash management system. It allows you to make better choices with your cash by using behavioral principles like Parkinson's Law so you spend less money to do the same things. As such, you will have more cash. Second, just because the term "Profit First" emphasizes planning for and ensuring profit, it does not mean you have to use it in the sense many people think of—buying flashy clothes and fast cars, etc. In fact, Mike suggests using up to 99% of your quarterly profit distribution to pay down debt.[43] You certainly don't have to pay down your debt that aggressively, and some advisors will suggest you do otherwise. Personally, knowing that my husband and I do not owe anyone anything feels better than a higher yield elsewhere would.

FANCY-FREE

ONCE THAT FINAL BUSINESS LOAN is paid off or you own your house free and clear, I want you to pause to enjoy how much lighter you feel. Look down and make a note of how far up Profit Mountain you've come. Take in the view. When next month rolls around and you have that much more money remaining in your Income account to allocate to the other accounts, I want you to recognize that amazing feeling, too. It is a BIG DEAL to be debt-free. Huge. But there is always a "but."

Before you get too cocky, let's not forget that good ol' Murphy (of Murphy's Law) is going to come calling with some unplanned problem. Here are a couple that happened to me in a matter of months during the spring of 2020. Two old AC units became nonfunctional at our house during the COVID-19 shutdown, followed by a broken AC unit at the office. Even though I didn't have to replace the AC unit at my office, I did end up having to close for almost a week because the temperature climbed to eighty-eight degrees inside, even with fans running and the back door propped open, before the part arrived and the repair was made. That meant another week of lost production and collections, which was on top of many weeks of the same thanks to COVID.

Thankfully, my husband and I keep a minimum of three months' worth of personal expenses in our personal bank accounts at any given time. There are no exceptions to this rule. For the business, as soon as my loans were paid off, the next landmark to pass on my journey up Profit Mountain was opening a fully funded "Vault" account. Up until the pandemic, I had never had a true Vault account, and none of my previous accountants or bankers had suggested it. And I rarely left 50% in the Profit account because I was laser-focused on paying down my debt.

I should have known better, but like most people, I never thought the worst would happen to me. I assumed that I would always be able to make more money. The COVID-19 shutdown taught me a very valuable lesson about the importance of having cash on hand.

CASH ON HAND (COH)

ONCE I UNDERSTOOD THE IMPORTANCE of having cash on hand, I needed to figure out a reasonable amount of money to keep in a low-risk, interest-bearing savings account that was easily accessible for two reasons only: in case of an emergency (like the ones mentioned above, where using money from the Overhead account would create a cash crisis), or when I needed or wanted to make a large purchase.

The rule of thumb is to have enough money to cover three months' (ninety days) worth of expenses. My Profit First Professional (PFP) banker friend, Greg Martin, would tell you that "Banks are more willing to lend you additional money, at a lower rate, when you have a sizeable amount of cash on hand."[44] I know it sounds illogical, but banks like to mitigate their risks and the best way to evaluate that is by looking at your current financial picture.

BARE-ASS MINIMUM (BAM)

OKAY, SO HOW DOES A dentist figure out how much money is needed to cover three months' worth of expenses? Well, first we need to calculate the bare-ass minimum (BAM) for *your* practice because it is most certainly *not the same for every dental office,* and it changes for your practice depending on how many employees you have and if you take on additional loans or, better yet, pay them off. The simplest way to determine your BAM is to find the total overhead expenses you calculated for your most recent year and divide it by 365.

Using the fictional numbers provided earlier for before and after cash management, you can calculate the daily BAM as shown below in Figure 9.2. The "before" overhead calculation yields a result of $699,570. When that number is divided by

365 days, the BAM needed per day is equal to roughly $1,917. However, if this dentist knows they will only have 200 working days in a year, the daily BAM should take that into account to determine what amount must be collected each day. Therefore, you divide the overhead number by working days (200) to get $3,498. The "after" overhead numbers result in a daily BAM of $1,573 and an actual working day goal collection BAM of $2,871. The BAM decreased by roughly $600 per working day now that all debts are paid off!

▷ BEFORE CASH MANAGEMENT OVERHEAD

Total Expenses from P&L	$949,457
Plus (+) Debt Payments	$80,627
New Expense Total	$1,030,084
Subtract (-) Previously Considered	
Doctor W-2 Wages	$258,000
Doctor Payroll Taxes	$15,360
Other Doctor Benefits	
Taxes	None
Interest Expense	$18,022
Depreciation	$7,304
Amortization	$31,828
TOTAL OVERHEAD	$699,570

$$\frac{\text{Overhead}}{\text{365 days}} = \$1,917 \qquad \frac{\text{Overhead}}{\text{200 working days}} = \$3,498$$

AFTER CASH MANAGEMENT OVERHEAD

Total Expenses from P&L _____ $574,149

Plus (+) Debt Payments _____ None

   New Expense Total _____ $574,149

Subtract (-) Previously Considered

   Doctor W-2 Wages _____

   Doctor Payroll Taxes _____

   Other Doctor Benefits _____

   Taxes _____

   Interest Expense _____

   Depreciation _____

   Amortization _____

TOTAL OVERHEAD _____ $574,149

$$\frac{\text{Overhead}}{\text{365 days}} = \$1,573 \qquad \frac{\text{Overhead}}{\text{200 working days}} = \$2,871$$

Figure 9.2: Calculation of BAM Using "Before" and "After" Financials

While using your overhead calculation from earlier will get you a quick answer to the "how much" question, it does not take paying anyone to do the actual dentistry into account. This is especially important to consider if you do not have enough COH at home to cover three months' worth of expenses and are therefore dependent on a steady salary no matter what. Also, if something happened to you (say you broke your wrist, for example), the practice would need to pay for a replacement or do without your production for a while. Once again, the doctor's salary needs to be included in the calculation to ensure you have enough funds to cover that kind of shortfall.

Therefore, let's calculate what I like to call the "drBAM" to avoid confusion with the BAM, which does not take the doctor's salary into account. Using the same numbers from the previous illustrations, you will see that the drBAM amount needed per working day is $4,865 for the "before" practice and $3,812 for the "after" practice. You'll notice the large discrepancy between the two; before cash management, the dentist was paying themselves more than "normal" via payroll *and* paying $80K annually toward debt.

▷ **BEFORE CASH MANAGEMENT OVERHEAD *AND* OWNER'S SALARY**

Overhead	$699,570
Owner's Salary	$273,360
TOTAL	$972,930

$$\frac{\text{Overhead}}{\text{365 days}} = \$2,666 \qquad \frac{\text{Overhead}}{\text{200 working days}} = \$4,865$$

▷ **AFTER CASH MANAGEMENT OVERHEAD *AND* OWNER'S SALARY**

Overhead	$574,149
Owner's Salary	$188,310
TOTAL	$762,459

$$\frac{\text{Overhead}}{\text{365 days}} = \$2,089 \qquad \frac{\text{Overhead}}{\text{200 working days}} = \$3,812$$

Figure 9.3: Calculation of drBAM Using "Before" and "After" Financials

VAULT ACCOUNT

ONCE THE BAM IS CALCULATED, you can easily determine what your Vault account should have available to cover ninety days' worth of expenses (that's ninety calendar days or roughly three months of working days). You, as a dentist, should never work for free, even in times of crisis. You have invested lots of time, effort, and money to keep your doors open, take care of patients' needs, and employ others. Therefore, I suggest that your Vault account goal be ninety days of drBAM at minimum. Using the numbers in the illustrations above, the practice Vault accounts should have roughly $239,940 for the "before" practice and $188,010 for the "after" practice to use strategically during an emergency and/or provide the financial flexibility to grow or pivot without affecting the day-to-day operations of the business.

My Vault account is the one account I set up at a different bank. I chose an online bank with no actual branch in my city. I do not even see or think about the funds in it until I upload the monthly statement to my accountant's portal. I continue to add money to the Vault account for three reasons: to keep the account active, increase the funds available for practice growth or new purchases, and build up my tax basis. Once I sell my practice, all the Vault account money will be mine, *all mine* (insert evil laugh). Even better, I will not owe any taxes on those funds since I was taxed when the profit was realized.

PLANNING YOUR NEXT STEPS UP PROFIT MOUNTAIN

Look at you! You know how to handle any outstanding debt, you can determine the BAM needed for each day you work *and* you now have a dollar goal amount for funding your Vault account using the drBAM, even if you don't have a Vault account... yet.

You are getting so close to summiting Profit Mountain.

So close.

It might be difficult to see what obstacles lie in the way of your progress or what path is best. Don't worry, I promised to help show you the safest, swiftest way to the summit and I've got you covered.

CHAPTER 10
BUILD A BETTER SQUAD

WHILE WE NEVER LEARNED MUCH about business in dental school, we did learn a bit about dental staffing. When I asked clinical professors and faculty what they thought was the hardest part about being a dentist, the majority of them told me, "Employees." So it seems obvious that a book whose sole purpose is to help dentists achieve a financially secure practice should include a chapter—or in this case, two—on what almost every dentist I have come into contact with since dental school has *also* said is the most difficult part of being a dentist and one of the biggest expenses you will have as an owner.

I will warn you that this is a *long* chapter, so please plan to stop along the way if necessary so you don't give up. I am including the key to the symbols that represent how much time I think certain tasks will take you as a reminder.

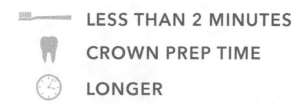

LESS THAN 2 MINUTES

CROWN PREP TIME

LONGER

Figure 10.1: Time Symbol Key

BUILD YOUR BENCH

Just in case you aren't catching on to the sports metaphor, I am referring to finding the right people for your office. They not only need to possess the right skill set or certification depending on the role, they must also get along with everyone else working under your roof and deliver the quality of care your patients deserve. Your employees are ambassadors of your "brand" and yes, your office has a brand. Every interaction between them and patients or other offices, whether by phone, email, snail mail, social media, or your website, contributes to your brand.

YOUR EMPLOYEES
ARE AMBASSADORS
OF YOUR "BRAND."

Those interactions must convey your core values and be handled professionally, with the right balance of enthusiasm, knowledge, and compassion. If you would be embarrassed if anyone knew a certain employee worked for you, then they should not be working at your practice. It is imperative to find the right people, or at least the *mostly* right people, who only need to learn a few additional skills to be proficient in their tasks.

DiSC™

DiSC™ IS A BEHAVIORAL ASSESSMENT TOOL.[45] The acronym stands for the four main styles of behavior described in the model: dominance, influence, steadiness, and conscientiousness. Learning DiSC™ behavioral styles can help you discover and take advantage of your unique behavioral strengths. This tool can also help you better respond to your team and patients.

Having taken personality tests back when my mother was earning her master's degree in counseling school psychology and when I was a college student trying to make sure my personality style matched up with any professions I might be considering, I've known for a while that there is value in learning more about the differences between people and their inherent personality traits. The DiSC™ model was first proposed in 1928 by William Moulton Marston, a physiological psychologist, inventor, and the creator of Wonder Woman. In his book *Emotions of Normal People,* he chose to focus on behaviors, since those can be directly observed and objectively measured.[46]

I learned about DiSC™ at a leadership seminar in 2017. I have since taken the assessment a handful of times, and my score always has me as a CD, since my behaviors very strongly align with the traits of conscientiousness and dominance. While that means that I am matter of fact and driven, as well as a good blend of introverted and social, it also means that I tend *not* to be receptive to new ideas, nor will I ever be the biggest cheerleader for my staff. I am truly thankful for my team members' dependability, problem-solving skills, and all they do for patients, though I likely do not tell them enough. This is not because I don't notice or appreciate their skills and gifts; it's simply *not my behavioral style*. I'm so goal-oriented that I expect tasks to be done correctly. Pausing to recognize what I consider basic requirements for proper job performance seems frivolous to me. However, many team members seek approval. They depend on their boss's confirmation of a job well done, and positive reinforcement of good behaviors, to keep motivated and engaged.

If you want to take a minute to determine your DiSC™ behavioral style, head to drjuliewoods.com and choose the link for "behavioral style."

Write your style here:

_____

Do you agree with the assessment? ___ Y ___ N

HOW TO USE DiSC™ WHEN HIRING

SEVERAL YEARS AGO, ONE OF my colleagues, Dr. Teresa M. Scott, shared with me how she uses techniques like those outlined below to get the right candidates to apply, then uses the DiSC™ assessment to further narrow down her hiring pool. Potential employees fill out an assessment as part of their application, and Dr. Scott purposely weeds out the people with strong D behaviors right away. She explained, "I can't work with a strong D at all. I know this about myself, so I won't even consider them." She went on to say, "You have to know yourself for this to work for you. However, since most dentists are detail-oriented, the following employee temperaments will likely work for you. I hire in order of preference: CS, CD, C, S, SI, then IS. I prefer IS/SI for hygienists and CD/CS/S for assistants and administrative team members."[47]

HIRE SLOWLY

THERE IS A REASON THIS advice stands the test of time and applies to all businesses. You must pay attention to the details in this process, starting with the job listing and up to the moment you offer the position to a candidate. I have broken down the hiring process into the following six steps so that you can refer to this checklist when you are trying to fill a vacancy.

1. **Craft a good job description** – To attract the right candidates to submit resumés for your review, you will need to include the pertinent details of the open position, hours to be worked, ideal years of experience, and the certifications required to apply. You should describe *why* the applicants would *want* to work at your office, for you, and with your team. Highlight the positives of your hours

and/or benefits and make sure to state the range of the hourly pay rate. Let them know your team is "drama free," if that's true. Once the job description is crafted, you can upload it to job listing websites and send it to any nearby dental training centers. I live in a small enough city that when the team and I have shared the news via text or social media asking for those interested to email a resumé, we have received many good candidates.

2. **Review resumés in a timely fashion** – You will often be in a time crunch to get a position filled, either because your employee is leaving within two weeks or they simply didn't come back from lunch one day. While I will remind you to slow your roll so you can be selective in your hiring, I don't want you to miss an ideal candidate because you did not respond to their email within twenty-four hours. A quick review of the resumé should give you an idea about the applicant's attention to detail, previous job longevity (job-hopping versus staying longer-term), skills, education, and any certifications that would be pertinent to employment at your office. At that point, you could ask for three reasons why they think they make the perfect candidate for your position and/or have them fill out a DiSC™ behavioral assessment.

3. **Do a background check** – The first step of a thorough application review is running a background check on a prospective employee. If the open job is for any administrative position that will involve the exchange

of money or entering payment details into your patient software, I also suggest you run a credit check. You *cannot* run these reports without the candidate's written permission. I am lucky enough to have a reputable human resources (HR) firm across the street from my office. I keep a digital copy of the informed consent form they use, and once an applicant has signed off on the background and/or credit checks, I upload a copy of the document(s) and have the HR company run searches. They will suggest broadening the parameters of the search if it appears the candidate has lived out of state. Most of the time, I have results back within twenty-four hours.

4. **Ask for references *and* call them** - If there are no red flags that pop up on the background or credit checks, I see if the applicant included references. If not, I ask the candidate to supply three references that can speak to their work ethic and job experience. If the person is young enough to be unsure whom to use as a reference, I let them know that I will call their most recent employers or instructors. As a courtesy, I ask if there is any reason I should avoid speaking to their current employer (for instance, if their current employer does not know they are looking for a new job). If they request that I not call that employer, I ask them what they plan to do if they are offered employment with me or someone else. Their response gives me insight into whether they plan to give proper notice. The way they speak of that job and boss is also useful information to glean.

When I call a reference, I much prefer to call the actual place of business, as opposed to a phone number provided on the application or resumé, so I know I'm not calling a fake reference. I always explain whom I am calling about and what position the applicant is competing for. I then ask three simple questions: 1. Can you speak to this person's punctuality and dependability? 2. What is one thing that stands out as a positive about this employee? 3. If you had an opening in your office for an employee, would you consider rehiring this person? Sometimes you don't even really need to ask all three questions. *I've learned that it is important to note what isn't being said as much as what is shared.*

When I receive these calls on behalf of former employees, I keep it super simple and short if it's about an employee whose employment was terminated, or if they were unreliable, or if they could never quite live up to the expectations outlined in their job description. If it's someone I was sad to see go who was a consistently hard worker and team player and gave me proper notice when leaving, I will make sure to express all of that to the person calling.

5. **Schedule an interview** – If a candidate makes it this far, with a resumé that catches your eye, a clean record, and former employers that would rehire them, it's time to schedule an interview. Having done interviews in many different ways, my preference is to have the interviewee come in during a workday so they can meet the entire team and vice versa. This allows all of us to get a rough idea of how this person might fit within our office and how patients

might perceive them. It also allows the candidate to see us in action and witness the flow of patients in and out, the procedures we do, what we wear in terms of personal protective equipment (PPE), etc. Even when an applicant is currently employed, they can often leave for lunch, so in many cases they shouldn't have to ask for time off. If they absolutely cannot come in when everyone is working, the next best thing is to meet with them individually. During the early stages of the pandemic, I might have agreed to an online interview using Zoom or FaceTime, but I would not do so now. Nor would I consider a phone interview. Dental workers must be in the office, so it's a no-go for me if an applicant is unwilling to come to our office for an interview.

6. **Extend an offer** – By the time I am ready to extend an offer of employment, I already know I am willing to take on the risk of hiring this candidate. Since most of us crave clarity, my intention with the actual offer is to set expectations for the employee. I will have gone over the basics of these points more than once, in the job listing and at the interview, but an offer letter provides a written record of exactly what I am promising them if they agree to the terms and accept the position.

   A well-crafted offer letter includes the hourly wage, the number of hours the employee is expected to log weekly, the benefits offered and their timing (for instance, new hires must wait a year before they are eligible to participate in our retirement plan), which holidays are paid, how much paid time off they will accrue and when they can use it, the date of the first day of employment, etc. Things to consider regarding compensation and benefits will be discussed in the next section.

IF YOU HAVE NOT FOUND THE RIGHT APPLICANT, *KEEP LOOKING.*

There will be times when you are tempted to make an offer to anyone who has a pulse and can hold a saliva ejector. *Hire slowly.* Go through steps one through five above, and if you have not found the right person, *keep looking.* Don't be tempted to extend an offer to someone who doesn't represent your brand well or doesn't seem to be a good fit with your team. You can get by with fewer people until you find a better applicant. You can do hard things.

COMPENSATION AND BENEFITS

EVEN THOUGH I'M NOT THE greatest with praise by social media standards, I am a generous employer. I'm sure some would say I'm "too nice." I have read awful things that make me aware that all employers are not the same. Many dentists and DSOs do not respect the people they employ, nor will they ever have empathy for the economic hardship caused by low wages or a lack of benefits.

Before I hire anyone for a new position, or when I put together information to go over at the time of annual employee reviews, I do my homework in terms of wages. I check online to ascertain the range for that job within our area. I rarely offer a wage at the low end of the range, even if someone has minimal experience. I want to attract and keep good employees. When I first became an owner, most employees were only concerned about the hourly wage they might expect. Over the years, I have seen more questions and appreciation regarding other benefits.

Employee: _____ Position: _____

Current hrly wage: _____ Time frame evaluated: _____

    Annual wages _____

    Annual payroll taxes _____

    Paid time off (ex: vacation, sick days) _____

    Paid holiday time _____

    Retirement contribution _____

    Continuing education _____

    Travel expenses _____

    Insurance premiums _____

    Uniform allowance _____

    Other benefits (ex: meals, free dental work) _____

Total compensation: _____

Hrs worked during time frame: _____

Adjusted hrly wage (total compensation/hrs worked) = _____

Figure 10.2: Example Employee Benefit Worksheet

Links to find salary ranges
for employees can be found at
drjuliewoods.com.

GROUP HEALTH INSURANCE VERSUS STIPENDS

WHEN I WAS AN ASSOCIATE, my health insurance was covered by the business. As an owner, I have always placed value on offering health insurance as a benefit to all employees. However, the changes to health care coverage that resulted once the Affordable Care Act was enacted meant that many employees do not have to rely on a spouse or an employer to procure health insurance coverage. Also, as an employer, I can have a "group" plan even if I am the sole member of the group. When I first began writing this book two years ago, my team was a mix, with roughly half who wanted to be on the employer health plan and half who preferred to receive a health stipend, since I offer one or the other. Over the course of these last two years, my staff has changed and the cost of health insurance premiums has gone up 25–100%. So I reevaluated that expense and researched all of our options for coverage. For 2023, I am covering the cost of health insurance provided through Farm Bureau Financial Services. Unfortunately, that may not be an option for you as they only have agents in fourteen states.

This situation was a good reminder to me that *all expenses* need to be reevaluated at least annually to make sure that better solutions aren't available. Switching our insurance will save the business roughly 25% of the premium costs from the previous year! That allows me some flexibility to offer a small hourly increase to my employees if I choose and not be out any additional money.

Those who receive a health stipend get a fixed amount every pay period. It's always less than I pay toward other employees' premiums because the stipend is considered a wage. As such, I also have employer taxes to pay that increase the amount of cash that leaves the practice. Dental insurance is an option for the team members who are part of our group plan, and many opt in to that since I am not a general dentist and therefore cannot take care of their restorative needs. I do allow my staff to have dental radiographs, routine periodontal maintenance, and prophies done at my office. Direct family members, the definition of which is found in my employee handbook, also receive a 20% discount off services provided they do not have dental insurance.

PAID TIME OFF VERSUS VACATION AND SICK LEAVE

OF IMMEDIATE CONCERN TO NEW hires is whether they get any paid vacation time and can choose what days they want to be off work, and how they will be compensated if the office is closed at other times. When I was a new owner, there was a certain amount of time allotted for vacations, sick leave, and paid holidays. I still pay on the same six holidays, whether they fall on a working day or not: New Year's Day, Memorial Day, July 4th, Labor Day, Thanksgiving, and Christmas. However, everyone now gets a certain amount of paid time off (PTO) to cover time spent on vacation, when home sick, when a child is sick, or when we close due to power failure or an "ice day," etc.

When someone wants to be away on a day that the practice would otherwise be open and I am scheduled to work, they must submit a request for time off. If more than one person in the same position wants off, then the person who requested to be off first will get the day off.

I think I already mentioned that I rarely work more than 150 full days a year in the practice anymore. I do not automatically close the office down when I am out. Thankfully, in Kansas, hygienists can still see patients when I am gone if I have seen the patients within the past twelve months. That allows for patients to be seen and workers to be in the office regardless of my presence in the office. I printed out those dates and placed them at each computer so, when it's time to schedule regular periodontal maintenance appointments, those weeks can be booked with patients I have seen at their most recent appointments. Not only does this ensure that we schedule those weeks with the ideal patients, it also leaves time in my schedule to see the patients I must check or who need anesthesia.

I prefer to have at least one person in the office Monday through Thursday during our normal business hours to take calls from referring offices, answer patient calls, follow up on unpaid claims, etc. There is almost always something for staff to do if they want to be in the office. The only times I do *not* allow anyone to be in the office when I am also gone is when the weather makes getting to or from the office dangerous, and on the days immediately before and after Thanksgiving and Christmas, when most dental offices in the United States are closed.

I know there are offices where the dentists determine what days they will or will not see patients for an entire calendar year, and their staff is expected to take the same time off and schedule all personal appointments—physician appointments, oil changes, trips to the veterinarian's office, school volunteering times, etc.—when the office is closed. I have found that my employees' needs often do not match up with mine, so I think it's a bit unfair to demand that they schedule their lives around what works best for me. Again, there is no wrong or right answer to what your policy should be. Nor is there a standard amount of PTO offered by most dental offices. One of the responsibilities of being an owner is determining what is best for *you*, your employees, and your patients. Sometimes you will have to alter your policy based on current market trends. Whatever you choose, make sure the parameters are properly documented in your employee handbook.

When possible, I try to approve any requests for PTO when they're made at least three months in advance. When someone needs a more immediate accommodation, for example, only one or two hours so they can go to their child's awards ceremony or attend the funeral of a close family member, I try to use the Golden Rule to guide my behavior when feasible.

Some dentists will not move patient appointments even when they are sick or in so much pain that they should seek emergency medical attention, much less for something as "trivial" as a child's performance in a school play or a colleague's funeral. However, I always keep in mind that patients would not hesitate for one minute to cancel on me for the same reasons, or for reasons even less pressing, like a hair appointment they forgot. I have yet to hear of anyone at death's door saying they wish they had worked more. When you need to, or even when you want to, *move the patients and go!*

OTHER BENEFITS TO CONSIDER

I HAVE KNOWN SINCE I first decided to be an owner that I wished to be the kind of employer that *I* would want to work for. That meant I wanted to pay an above average wage, pay for uniforms (aka scrubs), and offer health benefits and retirement. I knew I wanted my employees to learn about new procedures and I hoped I would be able to afford to pay for their travel to some of the courses. "Scratch owners," those who start their own practices, often don't have the luxury to do these kinds of things. All owners should have discussions with their accountants about what they can reasonably afford to do and what they want to offer, and make decisions based on both the financial reality and core values of their practice.

EMPLOYEE ONBOARDING

PROPER ONBOARDING OF ANY NEW hire is crucial to their success. It would be unfair to get frustrated with someone if they have not been taught how to do something the way you expect it to be done. I ask new employees to arrive on their first day with two forms of acceptable ID, which are necessary to comply with Internal Revenue Service (IRS) requirements for working in the U.S., and a voided copy of a deposit slip. These days, some employees do not even have deposit slips, in which case I have them bring in a document of some kind that has their bank routing number and account information for me to keep on record. They are given a copy of the federal W-4 form to fill out and the equivalent form from the state of Kansas. With their deductible information and the terms of the job offer, I can easily get them set up for payroll.

When they return the forms to me, I hand them a copy of our employee handbook and take them to the employee breakroom, where it's quieter, so they can concentrate. They are instructed to carefully read over everything in the ten-page handbook so they can follow up with any questions. Years ago, I worked with HR Partners of Kansas to make sure all the pertinent information was included and up-to-date. Mobile phones and social media are examples of topics we did not even have to address when I first took over as an owner in 2006. I highly recommend that you get a local HR company, and/or one that is intimately familiar with the labor laws of your state, to help you draft your employee handbook. In Figure 10.3, I have listed many of the main topics your handbook should address.

HANDBOOK TOPICS

INTRO

Purpose of Employee Handbook
Nature of Employment-At-Will Statement
Equal Employment Opportunity
Immigration Law Compliance
Disability Accommodation
History/Culture of the Practice

WORK CULTURE

Employee Relations
Personal Relationships in the Workplace
Open Door Policy
Business Ethics and Conduct
Confidentiality
Non-solicitation
Social Media
Access to Personnel Files
Telephone Etiquette
Personal Cell Phone Use
Dress Code
Company Property
Outside Employment
Visitors in the Workplace
Information Security

EMPLOYMENT

Introductory/Orientation Period
Payment of Wages
Pay Deductions
Administrative Pay Corrections
Timekeeping and Reporting
Work Schedules
Meal Periods/Break Periods
Overtime
Travel and Reimbursement

BENEFITS

Holiday Pay
Paid Time Off (PTO)
Jury Duty (Paid/Unpaid)
Bereavement Leave (Paid/Unpaid)
Health Insurance
Dental Benefits
Retirement
Continuing Education

PERFORMANCE STANDARDS

Performance Reviews
Attendance and Punctuality
Progressive Discipline
Problem Resolution
Salary Review

SAFETY AND SECURITY

Drug and Alcohol Policy
Parking
Personal Use of Vehicles
Workplace Violence Prevention
Workers Compensation
Tobacco Use/Tobacco Free Workplace
Emergency Closings
Inclement Weather
Accident Reporting (OSHA)
HIPAA

TERMINATION

Termination of Employment
Final Pay

Figure 10.3: Main Topics to Include in Your Employee Handbook

There is a page at the end of our handbook where the new employee must sign and date an acknowledgment that they have read the manual. I also handwrite any topics that needed clarification on that page and have them initial that they understand what the handbook specifies about those items. I also sign and date the paper. That document, and the copies of the acceptable forms of identification and bank information, go into an employee file that I keep in a locked, fireproof filing cabinet. According to the Equal Employment Opportunity Commission (EEOC), employers must keep all personnel and employment records—including job applications, requests for reasonable accommodation, and forms I-9—for one year from the date of termination or three years following the employee's hire date, whichever is later.[48]

Check to see if you have an employee handbook. If not, check with local colleagues and get recommendations for a reputable HR company to help you craft one. If you have one already, make sure it's up-to-date with your current policies and that you have documentation showing that all your current employees have read it. If they have not, give everyone a copy and have them sign a new sheet attesting they have read and understand the handbook.

Before I bore new employees with more paperwork, I have them begin shadowing the person who is currently in their position. The existing employee explains things as they do them. If the employee who previously filled the position is no longer available to train a new employee or I do not want the new employee to learn from them, I have another cross-trained employee show the new person the basics of the tasks before asking the new hire to perform any of the duties on their own. I have found it to be far less overwhelming for new employees to observe for a while without the pressure of performing the actual tasks, especially if they are new to private practice or dentistry or just finished up a training program. Several of my employees have come from other fields, like a Lasik eye center, an OB/GYN office, and even an accounting firm.

At the end of the first day, I give the new person a copy of our procedure manual, which has tons of information for each position in our office. There are detailed checklists and instructions for all the daily tasks, plus information and photos about proper instrument setups; different surgical procedures that I perform, and the pros and cons of those procedures; post-op instructions; how to handle any kind of issue that a patient might phone about; and how to print monthly statements and change the outgoing voice message, etc. I make sure there are copies of this manual for everyone. Having this reference is especially helpful if a staff member is unexpectedly absent and someone on the nonclinical team has to help turn over rooms or take things in and out of the autoclave. The manual is also helpful when someone on the clinical team needs to help with answering phone calls, scheduling patients, or running checks through the bank scanner so money is deposited on time.

The best way to know if your procedure manual is detailed enough is to have someone completely unfamiliar with the inner workings of your office—for example, a teenage child, a spouse, parent, or non-dentist friend—try to perform the duties as outlined *without asking for any assistance from you*. If they can, the manual is ready to go until something fundamental changes (like when you switch from Televox to Solution Reach, for example). If there are any tasks they cannot complete without you, you will need to sit down with them and document the missing instructions. It would be a great idea for this manual to be reviewed annually at one of your regular team meetings.

Do you have a procedure manual?
If not, slowly begin to build one. Start
with one small task, such as how to set up
an operatory for a composite filling, and
have your assistant outline a rough draft
for you to check for accuracy. If you already
have a procedure manual, have your team
members review the section about their roles
and mark anything that needs to be changed.
Getting it completely up-to-date will take
longer than an hour, but starting somewhere
is better than not starting at all.

EMPLOYEE PERFORMANCE REVIEWS

DURING THE FIRST NINETY DAYS of employment, new team members get regular feedback as they proceed through training. Additionally, they participate in regular team meetings (which will be discussed in more detail in the next chapter). It's still critical to set aside time at the end of the first three months to formally review job performance with your new hires. I have found that the more regularly I have these meetings, the less intimidating they are, not only for the employees, but also for me! I found that when I didn't schedule annual reviews, they simply did not happen. Sometimes problems resulted from my waiting too long to schedule these meetings; in a couple instances, by the time I did meet with someone, I was so frustrated that it was difficult for me to refrain from being overly critical. It also led to uncertainty on behalf of the employees about whether they deserved a merit-based raise or one that was more in line with the increased skills or efficiency they were demonstrating.

I allow up to an hour for annual reviews. I like to keep them short and sweet. I fill out a form regarding the employee's job performance and give them numerical ratings corresponding with "needs improvement" to "excellent." I review that with them and explain their compensation and benefits worksheet (see Fig 10.2 for an example). Last, we talk about ways for them to expand their skills or knowledge and discuss what they might need from me or another resource to achieve that goal.

WHEN ALL ELSE FAILS, FIRE QUICKLY

I TOLD YOU THAT, WHEN I purchased the practice back in 2006, there was one employee I never even hired. This was because I knew from working with her as an associate that she would *not* be a good ambassador for my office and brand or a good fit for me and the rest of the team. It would take me almost *six years* to fire my next employee, and I should have done so well before I did. I have since fired numerous people. I think the all-time shortest period of employment in my practice was exactly thirty calendar days, or seventeen working days. With two instances of calling in sick during that short time frame, in addition to other issues involving job performance, I chose to terminate via phone and email on the second day she called in.

CORRECTIVE ACTION FORM

UNLESS AN EMPLOYEE BREAKS MY trust by lying or stealing, or consistently does not come to work, I like to give them an opportunity to improve their attitude or performance. That means I must give them feedback and a chance to make positive changes. Feedback is *not* always negative. In fact, the most helpful feedback will define any problem(s), including a description of why it's an issue for the practice, and offer solutions or corrective steps that can be taken.

When preparing for this kind of conversation, you might feel nervous or intimidated. I know I often overthink the upcoming interaction; I used to fret for days. I feel more prepared and confident when I have something written to reference. It allows me to organize my thoughts and remove as much emotion from the conversation as possible. I suggest you review the issue verbally with the employee and give them a written copy of what you review. You should document when the conversation happened and their response.

HUMAN RESOURCE (HR) CONSIDERATIONS

YOU NEED TO BE AN active listener to whatever information the employee conveys, but you do *not* have to make them any promises and, depending on their response, you can still terminate their employment if that's appropriate. However, even if you think termination is only a remote possibility, you should check with your state laws and/or whatever human resource firm you use to confirm what must be done ahead of time to make same-day termination possible. If I'm concerned that a day might turn into an employee's last at our office, I will schedule someone from the HR firm to come over and act as a witness to the conversation. Most of you don't have an HR firm across the street—in which case you can put another employee on alert that you might need a witness.

If it's an employee to whom I have given adequate time and warnings and still have not seen the changes necessary to move forward, then it's time to plan for termination of employment. Even if it's a new hire and they are still within their first ninety days, I *always* confer with the HR company to make sure I have thought of all the state-specific intricacies of firing them.

Countless times within social media groups, I have seen dentists voice their concerns about firing an employee based on the possibility of having to pay unemployment or getting sued. I have also seen instances where people have been worried because they live in a small town and firing someone in their office might not go over well with others. Over my sixteen-plus years of practice ownership, I have worried about many of the same issues at some point. I would like to reassure you that if you terminate someone within the parameters of your state laws, you *should not have to worry* about any negative consequences. As a small business owner, you have been paying into the state unemployment insurance fund each quarter, and when and if someone were to ever consider filing a lawsuit against you for wrongful termination, they would first have to find a lawyer willing to take on the case. You and your attorney would then use your documentation and the facts to argue your case—if it ever came to that.

I know that many of us have a bias toward giving employees ample forgiveness and time to change. Many of us also want to avoid confrontation as much as possible. That said, having tough conversations and making these types of decisions is essential to being a Dental Officer in Charge (DOC). Often, non-dental businesses offer severance compensation and benefits to employees to ease the blow of termination. I have certainly done so in some circumstances, and conferring with your HR resource is best for these situations. They can also help you prepare for getting the office keys and any other property back, figure out when the employee's last paycheck or direct deposit must be made, how to handle accrued vacation or PTO time, etc.

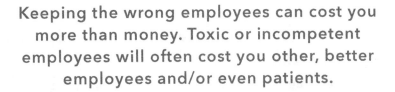

Keeping the wrong employees can cost you more than money. Toxic or incompetent employees will often cost you other, better employees and/or even patients.

The best advice I have received in terms of terminating someone's employment is to keep it as simple as possible. Even though you have plenty of reasons in mind as to why the employee is not a good fit for your team, keep them to yourself and do not engage if they want to know why they are being fired. If your team wasn't expecting you to let a team member go, I highly recommend that you have a quick, huddle-like meeting with them to apprise them of the situation and to reassure them that you considered what is best for the remainder of your team, and your patients, when making your decision and that you're thankful for all they do to support you.

Since I wrote this book to help you become more profitable so you can live the life you want to live, I want to remind you that keeping the wrong people as employees can cost you more than money. Toxic or incompetent employees will often cost you other, better employees and/or even patients.

YOUR TEAM = THE LIFE PRESERVERS OF YOUR PRACTICE

THE FLIP SIDE OF THE toxic employee is the one who becomes like family. I can personally attest that employees are not only ambassadors of your dental brand and your office, but also people you can rely on when times get tough. They will be one of the legacies you leave behind and can quite literally be the life preservers of your practice.

On a hot August day in 2016, I got a text that would change my life forever. All it said was, "Michael and Kim Perry were killed in a plane crash this morning." The previous weekend, the two of them had attended a CE course in Florida with two other couples. The small airplane they were in for the return trip home to Oxford, Mississippi, crashed in Alabama, killing all six people on board. For context, Dr. Michael Perry was a third-year periodontal resident when I entered my first year at Baylor College of Dentistry. He and his wife Kim had me over for dinner at their home to welcome me to Dallas.

I remember how shocked I was. How I stared at my mobile phone in disbelief. Others on the text thread began to ask the questions that were swirling in my own mind. "What? Where? What happened?" My former co-resident, Dr. Nathan Hodges, filled us in on some of the details he had learned. Long story short, many former Baylor periodontal residents applied for and received emergency dental licenses to coordinate coverage of patients until the Perrys' practice could be sold.

None of that would have been possible without Dr. Perry's superb team. While grieving, they kept the schedule full and helped each new surgeon acclimate to their multiple offices, equipment, and protocols. They literally kept the place running while we merely stepped in and performed the periodontal exams and surgeries.

I have told Chris Mills, one of Dr. Perry's employees with whom I have kept in contact, that none of us could have done what we did without Dr. Perry's entire helpful, well-trained staff. When I was chatting with her about this recently, she said, "Dr. Perry was a firm believer that no one person should hold all the keys to one task. He never wanted to have to close because someone was out. He is the reason we were all able to transition as well as we did."

I still think back to that experience when trying to ensure that my own team and systems are reproducible so that, if the need ever arises, my team can carry on without me. I have also created a document for my team that includes the important numbers to call in case of an emergency. The main people your team would need to contact are your spouse or attorney if the emergency involves your spouse too. The next most important person to contact is a local dentist, or specialist, you trust to organize coverage of your office until you return and/or your office could be sold.

EMERGENCY CALL LIST

Spouse
Attorney
Trusted local dentist to help with coverage
Banker
Accountant
Insurance agent
Landlord

Figure 10.4: Emergency Call List

This kind of team, the true all-star squad, does not happen magically. Nor is it a guarantee, even if you follow all the steps and consider all the elements mentioned in this chapter. It can be very difficult to retain long-term employees and *not* become emotionally attached to them. I think it's normal to be invested, both financially and emotionally, in your employees. In the next chapter, we will look at how to foster team spirit and "groupthink" so that you can perform the highest tier of service for your patients.

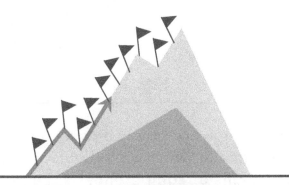

CHAPTER 11
RETAIN THE RIGHT TEAM

EARLIER I ALLUDED TO THE fact that even if you hire all the right people, it will still take time and effort to build the team as a whole and then retain them. While a steady long-term team is a goal for many of us, cultivating this can be emotionally taxing. Sometimes it is because you have team members stuck doing things in one way. After all, it's "the way we do it" and they are resistant to change. Other times, it can be draining because these people become like family, and we all know family dynamics can be tricky. Just think of all the stories you have heard about gatherings over holiday tables. As dysfunctional as families can be, it can be incredibly difficult when a family member leaves or dies, and the same is true of long-term employees.

When it was time to write this chapter, I was smack dab in the middle of my own employee crisis. I was intimidated to the point that I was essentially paralyzed. I felt like such a fraud. Hello, imposter syndrome.

Imposter syndrome is a psychological occurrence in which an individual doubts their skills or competence to the point that they feel like a fraud.

Thoughts would come in and out of focus in my mind, but *I could not write.* I found it difficult to organize what I wanted to share. AJ Harper, my writing mentor and developmental editor, had taught me, "First drafts are all about math."[49] In other words, I needed to get words on paper. Get my word count up. The proper sequencing and editing could be done later. Logically, I knew this was true, but my inner critic was winning the fight over my headspace. I was anxious, but I knew I wasn't the only one with big changes happening within their team. We were deep into the Great Resignation at that point. I suppose I should consider myself lucky that it affected my office much later than those of many of my friends and colleagues.

We were down a hygienist and an administrative person and had been running assisted hygiene for over a year, while I had to see almost all the scaling and root planing patients, which had not happened since I became an owner. And we had been making do on the admin side by splitting up the duties. My whole crew, including me, was running on fumes. We were tired. We needed a chance to sit on the "bench," catch our breath, and let someone else sub in.

I at least felt hopeful. I had hired a hygiene student who had interned in our office, working as a hygiene assistant every Monday morning for months. She would be miles ahead of previous new hires because she had already spent time with us, met patients, and learned how our dental software worked, how to record probing depth and chart notes, how to schedule patients, etc. I was counting down the days until I could finally say, "Don't schedule any more root planings on my side. New patients will have to wait until we have an opening on the hygiene side."

Turns out, I would have to wait a little longer than I expected.

One Thursday afternoon, while I met with representatives from Big Brothers Big Sisters who had come to ask for a sizeable donation, my hygienist left a template-formed, impersonal resignation letter on my desk chair. Before I finished my meeting, she slipped quietly out the back door. I was shocked, angry, and sad. She had been with me for six years and the best I got was a Dear John note on my chair!?! To her credit, she gave me five weeks' notice, which was essentially unheard of since the pandemic began, and she helped spread the word about the position to potential applicants. I had a replacement hired in just over two weeks. Crisis averted—or so I thought.

Within ten days of receiving her Dear John letter, my surgical assistant of eighteen years delivered the news of her resignation in the middle of a team meeting. I didn't think anything could shock me more than the letter on my chair, but I was wrong. I was dumbstruck. Even now, my shoulders tense up as I recall that moment. To say it was awkward would be an understatement. I felt like a wounded animal. Hell, I was. I fought back tears and finished the rest of the day. I cried so much that night I was concerned about how swollen my eyelids would look at the office the next day. This felt personal. I felt betrayed. I was so nauseous the next day, I skipped lunch. I really wanted to go hide in my car, but I knew that wouldn't send a good message to the rest of my staff.

The deadline to submit this chapter allowed me to focus on all the knowledge and experience I had to share, which helped me remember that I was not a fraud. In fact, I had kept most of my employees longer than many of my colleagues had managed to retain theirs. I knew how to make a cohesive team. I had perfected the art of getting rid of poor performers and toxic employees. My continuing education track record showed that I consistently took courses to learn how to manage the most difficult part of being a dentist—employees.

Remember, teams don't magically form and stay together forever. Take one look at any collegiate or professional sports team to know the truth of that last sentence. And, much as with the content of the last chapter, absorbing all the information I plan to share with you over the next several pages won't guarantee you will love every day with your employees for the remainder of your time practicing. However, I do hope that all these words I finally got down on paper will serve as a reminder that there *are* actionable steps you can take to make your team better, which will in turn lead to more stability for your practice.

BUILD UP EACH EMPLOYEE

Many dentists I know balk at the idea of paying for team members to learn new things since they might leave. They hire them to meet specific job requirements and train them to perform those duties. I think it's prudent to cross-train and/or at least better prepare your employees for their *next* job.

Hear me out. I'm not the one who came up with this idea. I have seen it in memes across the internet that go something like this:

WHAT IF WE TRAIN OUR EMPLOYEES AND THEY LEAVE?

WHAT IF WE DON'T... AND THEY STAY?

While researching this book, I found that many suggest this is a riff on the following quote from the founder of the Ford Motor Company, Henry Ford: "The only thing worse than training your employees and having them leave is not training them and having them stay."[50] Richard Branson, British billionaire, entrepreneur, and founder of the Virgin Group, has been quoted as saying about retention, "Train people well enough so they can leave. Treat them well enough so they don't want to."[51]

I have already mentioned how difficult it was when my surgical assistant of eighteen years handed in her resignation. I thought I had treated her well enough that she wouldn't leave. She, and others on my team, tried to reassure me that it wasn't personal—but that is not how it felt. As I mentioned before, *everything is personal* to a small business owner. After spending the appropriate time grieving, I reminded myself there was no possibility of advancement for her in my office, nor any wiggle room for an increase in her hourly rate. She was offered a 20% increase in pay elsewhere; I could hardly fault her for leaving.

As you likely intuitively know, it's not only the financial commitment of training an employee that can seem wasted if they leave, but also the investment of time and emotion. My friend and colleague, Dr. Rachel Hardin, asked, "How can I invest in new people without my heart breaking when they move on?" I inquired further about exactly what made it difficult. Her response: "Basically, anyone who works for me, I love them. It feels like a broken heart every time someone leaves."

I have seen countless others suggest distancing oneself from one's employees so as not to get too attached. Some of my female colleagues have stereotyped men as being naturally better at this. While talking with Dr. Jon McClure, I asked him what he thought about that and whether he had issues with the HR side of running a practice. He responded that employee issues weren't ever really a problem when he was the owner of his practice, and only blurred a bit once there was a change in ownership and therefore a change in practice philosophies. He described his team as "family."

The spectrum of owner relationships with employees ranges from compatible, cooperative, respectful, and sad when a "family" member leaves to authoritative, distanced, and detached enough not to be bothered as team members change. You likely feel differently about your staff depending on their years of employment, work ethic, and personality. I would like to reassure you that if you find it upsetting when team members leave, it will be okay. It's also normal to grieve.

Which is worse, though, retaining an average employee forever or keeping an all-star until it's time for them to move on?

TEAM MEETINGS AND HUDDLES

As you work on improving each employee, you also want to start making sure all your employees function as a cohesive team. If your office is big, this can seem especially daunting. One of the fastest ways to get people on the same page, and utilizing the same systems and language, is to have regular team meetings.

There, I said it.

You really do need to have recurring, scheduled, nonclinical time to meet with your employees.

Trust me, I can hear your groans in Kansas. I have been there, loudly sighing too. I used to be so busy producing more that I didn't have the time or energy to run team meetings. However, I found that when I don't have regular team meetings, the level of service we provide to our patients is not as consistent as I want it to be. Therefore, I highly recommend you make time for them during normal working hours *and* know that your team must be compensated for attending. Some of my clients pay a meeting rate for these meetings, CPR training, and/or hours spent attending off-site CE courses. I have done both, but for simplicity's sake, if the meeting or training is held in the office, I pay my employees their normal hourly rate.

When asked how much time I set aside for these meetings and/or how often I have them, I remind my clients that what works for me might not work for them. I suggest you try a few different times of day and figure out what works best for you and your practice. In my practice, I have found that what is most helpful for us is when we have two to three meetings a month that are roughly one to one and a half hours long. Trial and error also led us to hold the meetings at the end of the day. When we tried them over lunch, it took forever for everyone to eat or cut the chit-chat. In theory, first thing in the morning sounds good as no patient appointments will run late and steal time from the meeting. However, we found that many patients show up way ahead of their appointment times, and since we typically meet in our reception area, that was a problem. If you don't know exactly what to cover during the meetings or how to best set them up, you can certainly reach out to any number of practice consultants or talk with colleagues.

One of the most often overlooked and underutilized components of proper employee development and training is the morning "huddle." I have included some tips for this from Upstream Dental Coaching in Figure 11.1.

The goal of a dental huddle is to spend a few minutes coming together as a team to plan the day and discuss vital patient information, whether that is regarding their medical health, treatment presented but never agreed to, or even something personal such as the loss of a spouse. If you keep an actual football huddle in mind, some of the same principles apply: You review the next play, remind the team of potential problem players, catch your breath, and keep the energy focused on the game at hand. Huddles help your dental team anticipate any unforeseen issues or time crunches and deliver consistently great patient care and experiences.

Developing Your Morning Huddle System

The morning huddle is a quick meeting that prepares your team for what you need to know to have a productive day. This time is used to review patient care with the focus only on patients for today. Practice "care" should be reserved for team meetings. Use the following list to ensure a comprehensive huddle is created.

When writing any system, start with WHY the system matters to the practice. What is your team trying to accomplish and what are the expected outcomes? This way, your team has a compelling reason to adopt and use this system.

Below is a list of considerations when making your "HOW" in the huddle system:

1. Determine where and what time the huddle will take place.

    a. **Note:** most morning huddles can be effective in ten minutes or less regardless of the size of the team.
    b. Does your end time give you enough time to get the team back to operatories and ready to bring the patient back on time?

2. Does a sign need to be posted that will let patients know you're in a meeting? *No interruptions and the whole team should be present!

    a. *"Please be seated while we finish our morning huddle. We will be with you shortly. Thanks for your patience."*

3. Think about how the team prepares. When are chart audits completed to ensure that the team can show up ready for the huddle?

     a. What items, by department, should be collected and prepared for the huddle? See below for chart audit ideas by department.

     b. Will you use route slips for huddles? If so, who will bring these?

     c. Will you create a chart audit checklist document, such as a laminated document that could be used daily to ensure that everyone brings what is needed for the huddle? Ensure that everyone understands how to be prepared for huddling at an individual level. ***See Audit Ideas below

4. Is there more? What else have you done in the past that works and is important?

     a. Review what you've drafted to determine anything that's been omitted or skipped that is ALSO important.

SUGGESTED CHART AUDIT IDEAS

ADMIN	RESTORATIVE	HYGIENE
Financial arrangements for incoming patients	Outstanding treatment	Outstanding treatment
Past due balances	Clinical needs	Exams needed, where applicable
New patients	Relevant treatment today	Medical history or alerts
Connectors	Medical history or alerts	Family members due for recare
Emergency times	Family members due	Crunch times
Open times	Emergency time	
	Crunch time	

**Figure 11.1: Huddle Tips provided
by Upstream Dental Practice Coaching**[52]

On the advice of a practice coach, I implemented a team huddle early in my career. However, I was a single mom at the time, and the earliest hour I was able to drop off my daughter for daycare or a before-school program did not leave any spare time before our first patients of the day. Instead of restructuring our office hours, I had my team run the huddles without me based on the notes I had prepared the evening before on problematic times in the schedule or where to work in an emergency patient should one call. My lead assistant would then follow up with me on anything pertinent I needed to know about—for example, a team member leaving early that day or an administrative task I needed to take care of before the end of the day, such as approving a request for time off. I modeled this system after one created by a periodontist whose office I visited for a CE course. She could attend the huddle; she just didn't like to.

When we first returned to the office following the COVID-19 shutdown, we did not continue the huddle due to the need for social distancing and the limitations of our super small breakroom. We have since brought it back. I highly recommend you not only have one every day, but also attend it. A well-run huddle should take less than five minutes each morning and will save you many minutes of frustration.

Look at your schedule for the next six months and choose twelve times for team meetings. Block off that time in your software and have your scheduling coordinator move patient appointments if necessary.

QUARTERLY TEAM-BUILDING

IN THE PREVIOUS SECTION, I discussed the importance of team meetings. In place of one of those each quarter, I suggest allowing more time for a team-building event. While I had done some of them sporadically over the years—book discussions, vision boards, Taekwondo-style board punching, discussing our DiSC™ styles, etc.—they seemed to be more effective once I started doing them regularly. These team-building events should *not* all be outings that you are stuck paying for, although one or two of those per year isn't a bad idea.

My clients and colleagues offer the best ideas for such outings. Some of the most memorable ones I have heard about include an after-hours shopping trip to a shoe store so team members could choose a new pair of tennis shoes to wear to work, axe throwing, bowling, pedicures or spa days, a live theater performance, and a limo ride to a vineyard for wine tasting.

You can still leave the office for the kinds of team-building activities that no one on your team would consider an "outing." I think leaving the practice is ideal for this, actually. I encourage you to rent your home to your practice and invite your team over. Seriously, rent your home with the provisions outlined in Section 280A of the United States Tax Code also known as The Augusta Rule.[53] This law was established in the 1970s to encourage homeowners to continue renting out their homes for short-term events, like the Masters Tournament held in Augusta, Georgia. Before the ruling, homeowners were taxed on the money they received in return for renting out their homes as if they were rental properties and not personal residences.

If you choose to rent out your home, to your dental business or others, know that there is a fourteen-day limit per year and you must keep detailed records of when it was rented out and the fair and reasonable market rent you charged. You must also be able to prove that you are the owner of the private residence. For more information, you can find a link to Section 280A of the Tax Code in the endnotes section of this book. This is *not* considered a tax loophole if you adhere to the parameters of the code.

TAX TIP: The Augusta Rule, also known as Section 280A to the IRS, allows homeowners to rent out their homes for up to fourteen days per year without needing to report the rental income on their individual tax returns.

Spend your team-building time getting to know each other better. Learn more about each other's roles in the practice. Practice patient handoffs so everyone feels prepared when transferring patients from the reception area to the treatment room, then back up to the financial coordinator. Brainstorm ideas on how to wow your patients, or how to get referrals if you're a specialist. Have staff work in pairs or small groups to find the best deals on some of your supplies and see who can get the lowest price. Collect items for a local animal shelter, deliver them, and sneak in a little time to pet the animals. Review a new procedure or a new book. Make vision boards and share them. The possibilities are endless, and a quick internet search of "team-building activities" will help you find something that piques your interest if nothing above has. Have fun. Be the team leader, but also a team participant.

Don't forget to pay your team for these shenanigans. Yes, you must pay your team. You *can* pay your team a meeting rate, though most of the time I pay my team their normal hourly rate if the meeting or event is held within our normal working hours. My rationale is that most employees are counting on the normal hourly rate to cover their expenses. When we go out of town, or if we are doing something in addition to our normal working hours, I pay the meeting rate without hesitation. I do tell them that in advance, however.

Of the twelve meetings you scheduled earlier, choose four, roughly one per quarter, that can be designated for team-building. Set the timer on your phone for two minutes and write down ideas for your first event. Do a quick internet search if necessary. When your alarm goes off, you can move on to another task (unless you're enjoying this planning moment).

TEAM APPRECIATION

A STRUGGLE FOR ME IS all the appreciation days that happen over the course of the spring. I think hygienists get a dedicated week of appreciation. To deal with my shortcomings, I could put someone else in charge of remembering and purchasing for such occasions, skip them altogether, or do something in place of them. I have tried all the options and it seems best received when I make an acknowledgment near or on the day or days when other dental offices are doing it. It doesn't need to be extravagant, but if I don't do anything, it sends the message that I don't appreciate my employees. Social media only seems to exacerbate the negativity of not doing anything, so I have worked harder to participate. My squad makes the effort for me, every year without fail, so I try not to disappoint them.

Birthday celebrations at our office are low-key. The team, including me, split the cost of lunch from a restaurant of the celebrant's choice. We all eat together, at the office. No gifts are exchanged. For milestone birthdays, such as when someone turns forty or fifty years old, I pay for the decorations and we make the office festive. Patients can then help us celebrate the team member. For those big milestone birthdays, I do purchase a personal gift and/or experience. To keep it simple for tax purposes, I pay for that out of my personal funds. For the "regular" birthdays, I pay each team member the equivalent of an extra full working day's pay in the paycheck that includes their birthday.

The only work anniversary we celebrate is in July, when we celebrate the day I moved to Topeka and started working with Dr. Stone. Technically, that was two years before I would become the owner, so I guess it's more like we are celebrating the birth of the practice legacy, but you get the idea. Most years, we split a bottle of bubbly, or I have a cake baked or something else relatively small.

On the tenth anniversary, I started a new tradition. I gave every employee $100 for each year they had been with the practice. At that time, my surgical assistant received a $1,000 bonus, while my newest hygienist, who had started only recently, received a ten-dollar bill. My husband and I were dating at the time, but he helped me host a party for my employees and their spouses. For our fifteenth anniversary in 2019, I took my team to the fanciest restaurant in town for dinner and repeated the $100-per-year-of-employment bonus. I haven't yet decided how we will celebrate the twentieth anniversary, but celebrate we will!

Make note of the following in your planner:

- Dental Assistants Recognition Week – first full week of March

- Dental Hygienist Week – second week of April

- Administrative Professionals' Day (nonclinical team) – look this up; it's always in the spring, but the date varies from year to year

- Boss's Day – October 16

- Dentist's Day – March 6

See if anyone on the team would like to help you plan something to recognize people on their special day.

FOLLOW THE GOLDEN RULE

ANOTHER WAY TO SHOW APPRECIATION for your employees is to extend them some grace. In other words, recognize and accommodate for reasonable problems that will arise when you have human employees. I have two scenarios that immediately come to mind when I speak to other dentists about this—one involves a major life event, and the other is a seemingly small annoyance that could become a big problem depending on how it is addressed.

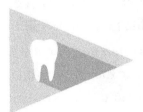

GOLDEN RULE: DO UNTO OTHERS AS YOU WOULD HAVE THEM DO UNTO YOU.

I wrote down what the husband of a colleague once told her regarding whether she should allow her employees time off to attend funerals or weddings. His advice: "Don't mess with life events." It's so simple, but I wish someone had said that to me early in my career to help me make the distinction between what is reasonable and unreasonable in terms of asking for time off.

The major life event involved for one of my employees was indeed a funeral. Obviously, she needed time off for the funeral, but before that, she also needed to help get her husband to and from appointments. She also needed some flexibility so she could stay home and rest after being up all night with him.

Fortunately for me, my team is cross-trained enough to cover for each other in this kind of situation. I understand that sometimes it just isn't possible, but when it is, do for your employees as you would like an employer to do for you.

Another example involves a much smaller issue—what to do when an employee gets a call from their child's school. To set the stage appropriately for this, I was a single mom with no family living in town for almost six years of ownership. I was the person who got the call from the school, and I had to get there as soon as possible to pick up my daughter. There is a single mom on my current team who occasionally finds herself in a similar situation. While she does have family in town, they cannot typically help her during the workday due to the inflexibility of their employers. When a call like this comes into our office, even for a clinical team member, they drive to the school to pick up their child as soon as it's feasible to leave and while a patient is waiting for local anesthesia to work or after new patient data is collected. Rather than leave for the remainder of the day, they bring their child back to work, where the child can rest in our breakroom. This works well for everyone unless the child needs to see a physician. If that's the case, the employee will go ahead and leave for the day. This allows the employee to take care of their child's needs and work as much as possible, with little disruption to our workflow. Again, I'm able to extend this flexibility because we have good systems in place and my team is cross-trained.

You have made it through two very tough chapters about building up your team, working together cohesively, and keeping everyone together. Bravo! You now have the tools to practice the way you want.

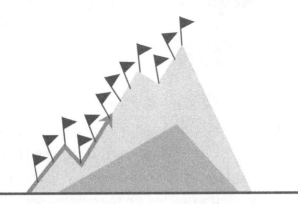

CHAPTER 12
CHOOSE YOUR PRACTICE DESTINY

WHEN YOU FIRST STARTED READING this book, you may have been struggling to add one more thing to your plate. But you powered through, hoping for relief or at least a plan to tackle the business side of dentistry. Or maybe you checked out this book because you wondered if implementing cash management and other systems might really increase your profitability. It might still be hard for you to imagine how on earth opening bank accounts and moving money around once a week will help you be more profitable. If you feel like I once did, you are desperate to feel better at work.

My unease and anxiety did *not* go away within the first week or even month of implementing cash management. There were many days when I wasn't sure that much had changed in my practice. I knew I had to do something differently, because producing more left me feeling awful, with no extra money to show for it. I wasn't going to make it another year if I didn't at least try. Before long, I found myself eating in the breakroom with my team more and more. Then I realized I was no longer crying as vacations ended and my Sundays were no longer filled with dread of a new work week. Even when I had minor setbacks, I found that being consistent led to small win after small win—until they added up to something much bigger than I expected.

This chapter is dedicated to helping you start down the path of practicing on your terms, using your values to guide your decisions. You get to decide what success looks like for you. The future of your practice is in your hands. *You get to choose your practice destiny.* Before I dive into any specifics, I think we need to pause for a minute and consider what might have led you to purchase and read this book.

THE PERFECTIONIST MINDSET

MOST OF US WERE ACCEPTED into dental school because we are high achievers with a single-minded focus on pursuing a career in dentistry. Dental school only reinforced these tendencies through the amount of time and attention that it demanded of us and the emphasis it placed on our skills being "perfect" down to the millimeter. We were rewarded for our hard work when we passed our written and clinical boards and then received the degrees that allowed us the opportunity to serve patients in our communities. Those of us who chose to further our dental education by attending advanced education or specialty programs knew we had to rank in the top 10% academically to even have a chance at acceptance into the programs.

As a result, many of us thought (and maybe still think) that the only way to be truly successful was to constantly do more and do it better than our peers. We got comfortable having to prove ourselves better than the person sitting next to us. Unhealthy comparisons between dentists began well before any of us were called "Doctor" and certainly before social media became a platform for bragging dentists with inflated egos. Even those of us who didn't try to one-up each other with our amazing dental talents or production were still all too eager to complain about our busyness. We wore it like a badge of accomplishment.

Maybe I'm naïve to think there was ever a time when people didn't celebrate how chaotic their lives were, but I certainly don't remember my parents carting us from one activity to another or missing family meals so they could attend meetings or stay late at work. Quite the contrary. We regularly ate dinners as a family on weeknights, and much of my activity involved spending time outdoors with neighborhood kids. That's not to say I didn't participate in Girl Scouts (I mean, I could sell the heck out of those cookies), play sports, or attend dance classes. I certainly did all those activities and more as I got older. Still, I never felt the need to "do more," and I never heard adults complaining to each other about how busy they were. Maybe they hid it better than we do now, or maybe being overscheduled wasn't seen as a positive thing.

Disconcerting research on how overachievers are likely to suffer from anger and disappointment due to their relentless pursuit of the next achievement can be found in *From Strength to Strength* by Arthur C. Brooks. It's worth the read, and I expect it will help you deal with some of the issues that seem to come out of nowhere but have been brewing all along as you bounced from one success to another. I was saddened to learn that all of us should expect "significant decline [in our dental skills] to come as early as our thirties, or as late as our early fifties."[54] Um, I didn't even begin practicing periodontics until I was thirty-two years old. I fell right in line with the timeline with disappointment and burnout plaguing me in my mid-forties, though. Thankfully, the author explains that if we kick our addiction to success and our obsession with overwork, we can avoid suffering through the second half of our lives. The key is not to bounce from one goal to the next.

Consistently working through this book and its action steps should ultimately allow you more time to figure out what makes your days easier and more enjoyable. I will warn you that solving your money issues will *not* automatically make you love running a business or lessen the stress of dealing with people. However, once you get your practice on the path to sustainable profitability, you will no longer be stuck on the production hamster wheel, fretting about the overwhelming urge to puke from the constant motion. You will finally have a little bit of time to pause and consider your options, with the most obvious decision being whether you want to keep practicing or leave dentistry.

If you grew up listening to The Clash, you may remember the song "Should I Stay or Should I Go"—and you're probably already humming the catchy lyrics that speculate about which option leads to the most trouble.[55] If you have never had the pleasure of hearing this song, I apologize for your inadequate exposure to legends of the eighties punk rock scene.

SHOULD I STAY?

STAYING WAS MY ONLY REAL option back in 2018. My daughter was finishing up sixth grade and I had zero intention of leaving my practice until after she graduated from high school. Plus, I still owed on my practice loans and the financial aid I had received to help offset my living costs during residency. I implemented the Profit First cash management system and learned to handle the business side of dentistry to get my practice in order. I began to spend more time working *on* the business to overhaul my systems so I didn't feel so out of control.

Many of you might find yourself in the same boat, where it doesn't necessarily seem like you have a choice to make. That being said, even if staying isn't your first choice, there are still lots of strategies to help you figure out how you want to practice dentistry.

TIME MANAGEMENT

IN EARLY 2018, I WAS exhausted from all that time in the operatory producing. I felt stuck in the practice. And when I first implemented Profit First and began taking back business tasks, I needed more time to accomplish all the new tasks of moving money, evaluating every expense, paying all the bills, double- and triple-checking payroll, etc. I knew if I didn't schedule time out of the office, I would continue to feel trapped.

At the macro level, one of the very first things I did was figure out with my husband when we wanted to have extra time together so he too could plan accordingly. I blocked out a couple of days every other month and scheduled one longer block out of the practice annually so we could travel outside of the country. I felt some relief knowing I had made time with my family a priority and had set aside specific time to spend with them. It was also a nice distraction to begin thinking about where we might want to stay and eat in southern Italy when we went the following year to celebrate Brad's fiftieth birthday.

Once those days were blocked off, I then looked at the schedule on the micro level. I reviewed with my team how an ideal day would be set up with a combination of exams and a variety of periodontal and implant surgeries on *my* side, and both periodontal maintenance and scaling and root planing appointments on the hygiene side. This helped with the physical limitations I have after practicing for many years, and it made the workload—and therefore production and collections— more consistent. I also made sure to block out time during the workday to work *on* the business so I didn't have to stay late or come in on Fridays.

NEW TEAM MEMBERS

ANOTHER STRATEGY I TRIED IN the beginning was adding an associate, with the hope that I could more confidently take time away from the practice without seeing any real changes to patient care or collections. I discovered it's not that simple to find a good match in an associate and it might be harmful to the practice if the person is not a good fit for your patients or other team members. It was definitely *not* the right choice for my practice, but some clients, friends, and colleagues have had better luck than I. This is something to keep in mind when you consider adding or subtracting team members.

Some dentists have had to add hygienists or hygiene days to cover all the patients who were absent during and following the height of the pandemic. While the price tag in some parts of the country can be daunting and prohibitive, a good hygienist who helps you offer comprehensive care to your patients can be a very valuable producer for you. Certainly, having enough time in your schedule to do the procedures that only you can do is worth it.

For over a year, my practice was down a hygienist, so I had to do almost all the scaling and root planing appointments. Not only was hygiene production down during that period; mine was also down since I had less time in the operatory to perform surgical procedures. While it was a necessary accommodation until more hygiene students graduated, I was thankful to get back to my ideal team size by adding back another full-time hygienist.

As I mentioned earlier, I fired some employees and had other, more natural turnover in employees who took jobs closer to home or for more money. If you have practiced long enough to make it through your first round of staff turnover, you know that some employees were not as good for you or your practice as you thought when they were still working with you. Others were great and difficult to replace.

There were numerous times after COVID-19 hit when my core team and I felt discouraged trying to recruit and train a new employee up to our standards. Several times, I had to follow the advice I give to "fire quickly." Thankfully, the crew that remains has always stepped up as needed to divide tasks and cover positions until we have a more pressing need to bring in an additional person.

I know so many clients and friends who feel like they're being held hostage by some employees. Those people need to be cut loose, even if it means everyone else does a little more in the interim. It's not good for anyone to feel like a victim, including you. On the clinical side, brainstorm with your existing team members on how to do things differently to accomplish your goals. Could you limit hygiene checks to only certain days each week? What about running assisted hygiene? Does your state allow for expanded function dental assistants? It is possible to get by with fewer people who are actually *on board with your practice vision* of the future so you don't have to be limited by poorly-performing employees' comfort zones? For administrative shortfalls, there are now outsourcing options for many administrative tasks, such as insurance verification, posting of payments, etc.

EVOLVE

PLEASE NOTE, I PURPOSELY DID *not* use the word "pivot." It triggers me, since so many "experts" told me it is the solution to all problems that have come because of the "new normal"— without giving specifics about *how* to pivot. I also want to make it clear that I am not suggesting you must increase your practice numbers, whether that's new patients or collections or even days worked in the office. Sometimes, it will be best to scale back.

I do believe it's healthy to keep moving and making small improvements, even as you encounter inevitable setbacks along the way. The best way for you to better your practice life will be very individual and based on your values and needs, which will influence your desires and goals.

I have zero intention of growing my busy practice any further. I am more than happy to be doing roughly 25% fewer surgeries without having it affect my practice margin. That is especially true now that I am completely debt-free. I would rather have more time within the schedule so I don't always feel rushed to the next patient or procedure.

I have also met my most recent practice goal of being 100% out of network as a provider for any dental insurance companies. I have every intention of submitting claims so my patients can maximize what few benefits they may have, but I am no longer beholden to what pencil pushers think is best for a patient. Now I am able to create a treatment plan based on what I see clinically, in the patient's mouth, as I am an expert in oral health. This was not a decision I made flippantly. I spent hours educating my team on the consequences of being an independent provider so we could prepare our patients for this transition. While many providers are nervous about going out of network due to the scarcity mindset that tells us we won't have enough patients remaining, it has been great to have the opportunity to naturally weed out the patients who don't value my experience and expertise. This is one of the most exciting changes I have made in my career.

Those of you who love a fast-paced, high-volume practice might choose to increase your marketing efforts, add associates or other employees, or even expand your physical space. That could be exactly what *you* need to fulfill your practice destiny. You might even wish to purchase another practice. Perhaps you will focus on wellness dentistry, airway issues, or clear aligner cases. Again, no one knows you better than you know yourself. There is no one right way to have a successful practice.

YOU CONTROL YOUR PRACTICE DESTINY. YOU GET TO DECIDE WHAT YOUR DEFINITION OF SUCCESS IS.

I will say it again for those of you who need me to speak up—*you control your practice destiny*. I will warn you, though, that even when you make the best decisions, there will still be days when you find yourself questioning the outcomes.

Many times over the course of my career, I have known without a doubt that I was unhappy, but found it difficult to pinpoint exactly what was leaving me wide-eyed after midnight with an unsettled stomach. Not knowing what specifically was making me anxious, I had no idea how to fix it. Working with Dr. Josie Dovidio through her Crown of Wellness program helped me retrain my brain so I was not only more aware of what was happening around me—both good and bad—but also how impactful it is to use my future vision to guide my present actions.[56] While it took some effort to sit with my thoughts and emotions and figure out exactly what I wanted personally and professionally, it has since made decision-making much easier for me, and with less second-guessing.

While I am less reactive these days, life still happens, and everything is *not* always fine! Often it's downright difficult. If it isn't trouble with employees or mean patients, it's water dripping from the ceiling or a car that won't start when my husband is due to leave for a twelve-hour call shift at the hospital.

The older I get, the more frustrated I become with how we have been taught to "be happy" or, at the very least, "fake it 'til we make it." Ironically, I was happy to stumble upon the book *Toxic Positivity* while I was in the process of writing this book. I felt reassured and *heard* when I read Whitney Goodman's words in the introduction about who the book is for: "people who are exhausted from pretending to be happy all the time—at work, at home, with their friends, and on social media."[57]

Guess what, it's okay to not love dentistry or decide you don't want to own a practice. There are physical consequences to constantly stuffing our emotions or discomfort and staying in relationships or jobs that aren't what's best for us. It is ultimately better for your long-term health, if you recognize that practicing is not in line with your values or needs, to either leave dentistry altogether or give up being a practice owner. Let's explore some of what you will need to consider if you decide it's time to go.

OR SHOULD I GO?

ONCE YOU HAVE DECIDED THAT something more drastic needs to be done, you will need to determine if you wish to make a quick getaway from the clinical setting, as your options for exiting will depend on that answer. I have watched numerous webinars on practice transitions and spoken with colleagues, CPAs, and attorneys on this subject. Most of them agree that it's ideal if you have a minimum of three years to prepare for your exit. Part of the reasoning behind that amount of time is that business evaluations are traditionally based on the past three years' collections. It will be advantageous for you to make sure those years have the dollar amount of collections you would like to see, since they will be used to determine the sale price of your practice, roughly 85% of the average collections of the most recent three years. That formula has been used for many years when selling private practices to individual owners.

In recent years, as more and more DSOs and private equity firms have purchased practices, offers have been based on the practice profitability and the EBITDA dollar amount as well as a percentage of collections. If you choose to sell to anyone other than another private practice owner, you will most likely be obligated to stay for two to three years and continue practicing dentistry. Again, that's why it is critical to determine how desperate you are to leave dentistry.

If you can hang on long enough to work *on* the business for three years before selling the practice, you can focus on making sure your collections are growing and on increasing your profitability. Higher profit margins will make your practice much more attractive to all potential buyers and lenders. I highly recommend that you speak with your CPA about ways to decrease the taxes you will owe on the sale of your practice by increasing the tax basis of your business.

I would be remiss if I didn't at least briefly mention several outside-the-office factors that should be considered when deciding whether to leave or sell. I think it is extremely important to look at your personal spending and debt, as well as all sources of income (or lack thereof) for your household. You will need to analyze your personal finances to the same degree you did your business finances to get a true sense of how prepared you are to go without your income for the immediate future, or permanently if you choose to retire. If you work with a financial planner, it is extremely important to share your plans with that person so they can help you determine if you have the cash flow necessary and are adequately prepared for future life events, such as the purchase of a new car or a child going off to college.

In addition to the financial implications of leaving ownership or clinical practice, there are also the mental, physical, and emotional aspects of a change of this significance to consider. Leaving a job, even if you have a zillion dollars and passive income coming in, is a big deal. It is a huge life change and one that registers fairly high on the Holmes and Rahe Stress scale, which compares life events in terms of how likely they are to increase your chance of getting sick.[58] Once you combine the other stressors that typically go along with such a change, you might reach the point where the likelihood of you getting ill is more than 50%. However, your health may already be negatively impacted if you stay in a job you hate or that causes you a lot of stress. If the decision to leave involves an illness or disability, please make sure to do all that is necessary to maximize your insurance benefits.

THE UNEXPECTED OFFER TO PURCHASE MY PRACTICE

IN THE SPRING OF 2022, I was approached by another periodontist about the possibility of selling my practice. I was very blunt about the fact that I had no intention of leaving for at least two-plus years, nor did I have any desire to bring in an associate in the interim. I told him that if he was serious, he would need to sign a non-disclosure and come to an agreement about the proposed terms of valuation, sale, and transition before I would even hand over any financials. In other words, he needed to agree to how we would evaluate the practice and he would share the cost of an evaluation, in addition to negotiating and agreeing to the percentage of the appraised value I would accept to sell. I found that I was far more protective of my practice than I had thought I would be at this stage of my career. My gut instinct was that he did not have any intention of purchasing the practice unless I was willing to give it up for less than its value. He confirmed that to be the case when he told my attorney he was only willing to offer 50% of the appraised value. As I knew the offer should be near 85% of the appraised value, I told my attorney I would rather risk not having a buyer in the future than sell it to a young colleague who showed little respect for me or the responsibilities that would come with taking over a well-established practice with a loyal patient base.

Thankfully, I knew enough to be leery of his intentions from the get-go and did not share any of my practice information with him beyond what is already public knowledge.

My feelings about the future care of my patients and staff surprised me even though Dr. Dovidio had warned me that I might experience a variety of emotions related to the legacy of my practice. She explained that some dentists only care about getting the most money out of the sale and making a hasty retreat. Other practitioners, as I discovered I was, were more concerned about the well-being of their patients and teams.

I did *not* sell my practice. I am currently practicing roughly 150 days a year with no plans to drastically change that anytime soon. My husband, Brad, has transitioned to covering trauma surgery for hospitals as locum tenens, which means he is home more than he works. I have intentionally blocked out eight full weeks in my practice schedule this year so I have more flexibility to spend time at home with him.

I still have tough days when all the things that can go wrong do. However, I have considered other options for employment and found that nothing else compares, in terms of the full package, to working the hours and days I want, with a team of employees I respect and enjoy, providing needed surgical care for patients who want to maintain their dentition. My job is fulfilling more than it is frustrating, and for me, the benefits of being the dentist officer in charge (DOC) still outweigh the cons. I expect my feelings to change within the next decade, not only because I will have been practicing for twenty-plus years, but also because of the changes that will happen with my parents entering their eighties and my daughter going off to college. For now, I'm thankful that it's my choice to stay or go.

THERE IS NO WRONG CHOICE

WHEN I ASKED DR. DOVIDIO if she had anything to add on the topic of practicing the way we want, she responded, "We all have a sense of what we want in life. We know we want to be successful."[59] She went on to remind me that "Unless you spend time reflecting on how *you* define success and can articulate what you really want, you will likely end up in a vicious cycle of stressful striving. How will you know you have succeeded if you have never truly defined success?" I pondered the "stressful striving" part and realized that that was exactly what I was doing when I was trying to outproduce myself each month and year, thinking it was what would make me "successful."

As my practice became more profitable, I found that my definition of success has very little to do with how much I produce or collect. I am much more concerned about the people I serve, whether they be my patients, employees, friends, colleagues, or family. The bottom line is, our worth as humans is not determined by how much dentistry we perform throughout our careers, nor by how many five-star reviews we have. You can practice dentistry for two years or until you're in your eighties. No matter what you choose, you will retain your worth.

I agree with Whitney Goodman that we should give up the pursuit of happiness and focus more on what meshes with our core values and allows us to experience the highs, lows, and all the in-betweens this life has to offer.

NEW ADVENTURES AWAIT

WHILE WATCHING *14 PEAKS: NOTHING Is Impossible,* a documentary film available on Netflix, my husband Brad relayed stories about these amazing high-altitude mountaineers. Brad was animated, excited to tell me about the quest of Nimsdai "Nims" Purja's goal to climb the fourteen mountains with peaks higher than 8,000 meters in less time than the previous record of seven years. I was intrigued enough by Nims' ambitious goal to watch the film myself. "If I can stay alive," he said, "I can do this in seven months."[60] Seven months. I could barely watch him trudge through the powdery snow of the opening scene without my stomach tightening and my heart rate starting its own climb.

I'm still traumatized from my first trip to the mountains. When I was ten years old, my family drove from College Station, Texas, to Ruidoso, New Mexico, for spring break. Having spent my early years in Mississippi and Texas, I was way more familiar with flat land, humidity, and the beaches along the Gulf Coast. My experience with snow was limited to what I saw watching *Frosty the Snowman* or cutting out paper snowflakes in science class. This would be the first time anyone in my family had ever gone downhill skiing, and we were excited. Even my older sister, a disgruntled teenager at the time, complained less about having to leave her friends behind.

We borrowed the puffy snow bibs, coats, and ski boots from friends. Our suitcases were filled with waffle-weave long underwear and more turtlenecks, socks, and sweaters than I had ever seen in our home. Once everything was loaded in the trunk of the car, we set off on the ten-hour trek through the most desolate western part of Texas, passing actual tumbleweeds along the way.

The elevation, and my anxiety, began to increase as we got closer to our cabin, while the roads got narrower and narrower. The two-lane road from Ruidoso to the actual ski resort was *quite* narrow, with no shoulders. On the way up, the car hugged the mountainside. Driving down, it always looked like we were mere inches from falling into the canyon below.

While we were at the resort, my sister suffered from a stomach virus that kept her up all night vomiting. The next day, she and my mother stayed back at the log cabin so she could rest. My dad and I had the whole day to ourselves. As I rarely had "shotgun" privileges, I was excited to sit in the front passenger seat of the car—that is, until we started climbing up that narrow two-lane road.

I was overcome with fear.

My dad suggested that I close my eyes or lie down on the seat.

I tried both. It wasn't enough.

I crawled onto the floor of the car and curled into a ball until we were safely in the parking lot at the base of the mountain. I repeated the process for the ride down.

The base elevation at Ski Apache is *only* 9,600 feet. The Nepalese climbers who signed on to help Nims accomplish his goal were planning to summit peaks of over 8,000 meters, or *over 26,000 feet*, almost three times that height! As if that weren't accomplishment enough, Nims planned to summit all fourteen in seven months.

Fourteen 26,000+-foot peaks in seven months.

While I have no desire to climb a mountain, I am in awe of the physical and mental challenges these climbers conquered. Not only did they need to be the best, the strongest, and willing to put everything on the line, they had to do so within very specific weather windows. Annapurna was the first peak on their list to summit and for every three climbers who make it to the top, one dies trying.

As the movie opens on the scene of a lone mountaineer walking along a snow-packed route, Nims instructs viewers, "Don't be afraid to dream big. You can show the world nothing is impossible." He named his mission "Project Possible." My eyes light up and my lips form a small smile every time I think about his positivity and confidence.

I'm a big believer in making things happen when the odds are stacked against me. While heights themselves terrify me, I am *not* afraid of having high expectations for myself. Looking back on my dental career, I know that part of why I felt so defeated was because I wasn't "mastering" the business side of dentistry. I was struggling not only financially, but also with managing my team and figuring out a functional work-life balance.

It's likely that if you picked up this book, you were struggling in some way as well. You may have been wondering why on earth you spent the better part of eight years pursuing your dental degree only to find yourself overworked and underpaid. You may have been hoping for a little pixie dust to make your practice magically transform. You most certainly didn't think you had the energy necessary for all the work and the climbing you would need to do, on your own, but if you have made it this far, you are further along than you realize.

By reading this book, you have set yourself on the path up your own mountain. You just have to keep going. Reward yourself along the way. Stop and take a look around every once in a while and notice the small changes. My first breakthrough happened when my lunch breaks were no longer spent alone in the car with a cheeseburger and a side of tears. Maybe yours will be when you no longer fret over payroll, or when you figure out your "ideal day" and get block scheduling up and running. Perhaps it will be when you can cut your supply expenses by 20%, or learn how to make better use of your existing team members rather than worry about trying to hire someone new. Whatever it is that makes you dread going into the office a little less is another scenic overlook on your journey up Profit Mountain. Pause a moment at each vista to take a mental picture for your highlight reel. Enjoy the view right where you are. Recognize that you are in a serene spot that you may not have even imagined existed before you reached it. Rest if needed.

While my circumstances were nowhere near as harrowing as those of the mountaineers of *14 Peaks*, nor were there any real time constraints on my uphill climb, I still felt an urgency to "go faster." I am inspired by the Project Possible team's willingness to veer off course to help a fellow mountaineer.

After summiting Annapurna and sleeping at Camp Four, the Project Possible crew learned that a member of another team never made it back down from the summit. That climber had been stuck on the mountain overnight, in what is literally known as the "Death Zone." The odds were against his survival, and in similar situations, many climbers are left to die. Despite the fatigue, fear, risk, and timeline of their own project, four of the Project Possible climbers, including Nims, headed back up.

Lifted one at a time.

Via helicopter.

Dangling from a rope.

Nims said, "Otherwise, he was going to die in hope."

They did *not* want that for their colleague. I do not want that for you. Thankfully, by reading this book and making some changes, you no longer have to "die in hope" either.

I was moved by the character of these climbers. They were exhausted and on a race against time as it was. No one would have faulted them had they chosen not to respond. Yet respond they did. They spoke of their fear of going back up, but they also knew they had to do it. Nims picked the "best of the best" climbers for a reason. He had chosen the men that he entrusted with his life. He purposely chose all Nepalese climbers for the three phases of the climbs. He knew this could help their careers. He hoped the Nepalese might finally get the international recognition they deserved for their climbing abilities.

If you have not yet seen the movie, I highly recommend it. Nims was on a mission. He said of the project, "This is about inspiring the human race." I know they have certainly inspired me.

With my own financial woes buried under an avalanche of better dental experiences, I am back to enjoying the actual dentistry: working on patients in a dental operatory. I'm happiest when I have a #15 blade in my right hand and a retractor in my left, as that means I am using the skills I learned in dental school and residency. Helping patients have more confidence in their smiles and improving their oral health has always been something that makes me proud. I never dreamed I would say this, but I also really enjoy working on the business side of the practice, too.

As unbelievable as it sounds now, I almost walked away from it all when I lost sight of why this profession can be rewarding. My practice was controlling me, and I was barely hanging on. Were you feeling as hopeless as I was? Were you burned out?

Look how far you have come already! Your eyes are wide open now. You have the tools to begin working *on* your practice. You have learned better ways to ensure financial stability. You no longer have to produce more to be successful. Now you know, even if you have lost your love for dentistry or feel confused, lost, burned out, or weary, it's possible to move forward. Feel better. Climb to the top of Profit Mountain. If I can do it, so can you!

As a dentist officer in charge (DOC), you have greater control of your business—and your revenue and expenses in particular. How will it feel to have financial security? Will you sleep better? Have more patience with your family, team, and patients? Will you have more time out of the office to pursue a hobby? Will you allow yourself to take time out of your practice to go on your dream vacation … and pay for it ahead of time?

I want you to be able to live the life you want *now*. The one you first dreamed of when you set your sights on becoming a dentist.

I want your business to succeed.

I want YOU to be the inspiration for another dentist.

I want private practice ownership to not only be an option for seasoned dentists in the future, but also one that young dentists want to pursue. Their practice journeys will be easier as we act as their guides and mentors. No owner should ever feel alone, as there are plenty of people who are more than willing to offer their assistance, encouragement, wisdom, and friendship along the way.

I cannot wait to celebrate with you on top of Profit Mountain. While the view out across the horizon may not be as stunning as from a 26,000-foot peak, the transformation of your practice will be as blindingly bright as the sun-dazzled, freshly packed snow. Adjust your sunglasses if needed and take time to savor this most recent phase of your dental journey. Don't rush off to conquer your next peak just yet.

Celebrate this success! Savor it.

No more stressful striving necessary.

You earned the time to spend figuring out what your next adventure will be. Now that you aren't trapped inside the walls of your operatory, producing more dentistry, you have time to do some daydreaming. Don't forget to dream big, for ***anything is possible.***

APPENDIX 1

PROFIT OVER PRODUCTION (POP), LLC
BALANCE SHEET AND P&L BEFORE CASH MANAGEMENT

BALANCE SHEET Before Cash Management	
ASSETS	**TOTAL**
Current Assets	
Bank Accounts	46,792.00
Total Bank Accounts	$ **46,792.00**
Fixed Assets	
Leasehold Improvements	258,385.52
Furniture	126,417.60
Equipment	118,440.88
Accumulated Depreciation	−502,056.00
Total Fixed Assets	$ **1,188.00**
Other Assets	
Goodwill	475,977.39
Loan Closing Costs	709.61
Accumulated Amortization	−333,479.00
Total Other Assets	$ **143,208.00**
TOTAL ASSETS	$ **191,188.00**
LIABILITIES AND EQUITIES	
Liabilities	
Current Liabilities	
Credit Card	25,000.00
Payroll Liabilities	48,679.00
Total Current Liabilities	$ **73,679.00**

Long-Term Liabilities	
Note Payable – Practice Purchase	113,871.72
Note Payable – Computer Hardware	23,941.25
Note Payable – Leasehold Improvements	124,870.03
Total Long-Term Liabilities	**$ 262,683.00**
Equity	
Capital Stock	1,000
Retained Earnings	−143,078.00
Net Income	−3,096.00
Total Equity	**$(145,174.00)**
TOTAL LIABILITIES AND EQUITY	**$ 191,188.00**

PROFIT AND LOSS STATEMENT Before Cash Management	
	TOTAL
Income	
Fee Income	963,051
Refunds	−16,690
Total Income	**$ 946,361**
Expenses	
Accounting and Data Processing	67,288
Amortization Expense	31,828
Bank Charges	11,662
Business Promotion	10,646
Contract Labor	3,194
Contributions	3,450
Depreciation	7,304
Dues – Non-Deductible	200
Dues – Professional	4,503

Insurance – Operating	8,504
Interest Expense	18,022
Lab Costs	2,719
Legal and Professional	4,291
Meals and Entertainment	1,775
Meetings – Professional	750
Miscellaneous	332
Office Supplies And Expense	32,497
Professional Supplies	108,053
Rent	33,600
Repairs and Maintenance	495
Retirement Plan Expense	3,576
Safe Harbor Contribution	17,266
Salaries – Staff	262,922
Salary – Doctor	258,000
Taxes – Payroll	31,012
Telephone	8,189
Training and Education	2,111
Travel and Conventions	11,561
Uniforms	2,142
Utilities	1,565
Total Expenses	**$ 949,457**
NET INCOME	**$ (3,096)**

APPENDIX 2

PROFIT OVER PRODUCTION (POP), LLC
BALANCE SHEET AND P&L AFTER CASH MANAGEMENT

BALANCE SHEET After Cash Management	
ASSETS	**TOTAL**
Current Assets	
Bank Accounts	
Income	5,000.00
Profit	2,211.86
Owner's Compensation	4,423.72
Overhead	12,165.23
Tax Reserves	3,317.79
Vault	130,000.00
Total Bank Accounts	$ 157,118.60
Fixed Assets	
Leasehold Improvements	258,385.52
Furniture	126,417.60
Equipment	157,960.81
Accumulated Depreciation	−542,763.93
Total Fixed Assets	$ 0.00
Other Assets	
Goodwill	475,000.00
Loan Closing Costs	1,687.00
Accumulated Amortization	−476,687.00
Security Deposits	3,018.49
Total Other Assets	$ 3,018.49
TOTAL ASSETS	$ 160,137.09

LIABILITIES AND EQUITY	TOTAL
Liabilities	
Current Liabilities	
Credit Card	13,584.82
Payroll Liabilities	0.00
Accrued 401(K)	30,758.09
Total Current Liabilities	$ **44,342.91**
Long-Term Liabilities	
Note Payable – Practice Purchase	0.00
Note Payable – Computer Hardware	0.00
Note Payable – Leasehold Improvements	0.00
PPP Loan #1	0.00
PPP Loan #2	0.00
Total Long-Term Liabilities	$ –
Equity	
Capital Stock	1,000
Retained Earnings	79,700.46
Distributions	
Personal	−1,372.49
Taxes	−83,435.97
Net Income	208,588.00
Total Equity	$ $ **204,480.00**
TOTAL LIABILITIES AND EQUITY	$ **160,137.09**

PROFIT AND LOSS STATEMENT After Cash Management	
	TOTAL
Income	
Fee Income	1,006,900
Refunds	−8,601

Merchant Fees		−11,372
Total Income	$	**986,927**
Expenses		
Team Expenses		
Assistant Wages		42,038
Administrative Wages		74,360
Hygiene Wages		127,214
Contract Labor Wages		1,652
Staff Insurance Benefits		12,439
Staff Retirement Plan		3,488
Payroll Taxes		18,610
Payroll Processing Fees		4,662
Uniforms and Laundry		4,819
Staff Recruitment		2,425
Total Team Expenses	$	**291,707**
Advertising and Marketing		
Advertising and Promotion		26,548
Total Marketing Expenses	$	**26,548**
Dental Supplies		
Dental Supplies		84,523
Hazardous Waste Disposal Fees		2,549
Total Dental Supplies	$	**87,072**
Lab Expenses		
Lab Fees		3,304
Total Lab Expenses	$	**3,304**
Rent and Facilities		
Rent		43,200
Utilities		2,461
Facility Repairs and Maintenance		1,065
Janitorial Expense		200

Security		906
Total Rent and Facilities	$	**47,832**
Equipment and Furniture		
Small Equipment and Furniture		744
Equipment Repairs and Maintenance		921
Computer Support and Maintenance		14,482
Total Equipment and Furniture	$	**16,147**
General and Administrative		
Legal		2,642
Collections		2,096
Accounting		16,700
Consulting		29,724
Insurance–Business		6,789
Licenses and Permits		1,661
Dues, Journals, and Subscriptions		968
State PTE Tax		1,000
Bank Service Charges		98
Continuing Education		1,109
Conventions and Seminars		2,988
Travel Expense		6,432
Automobile Expense		102
Meals		2,892
Office Supplies and Expenses		11,725
Postage		4,210
Telephone		10,403
Total General and Admin	$	**101,539**
Total Expenses	$	**574,149**
NET OPERATING INCOME	$	**412,778**
Other Income		
Interest Income		114

Total Other Income	$	**114**
Other Expenses		
Owner Doctor Compensation		
Doctor Wages		150,000
Doctor Payroll Taxes		11,784
Doctor Health Insurance		13,217
Doctor Family Wages		12,210
Doctor Family Payroll Taxes		1,099
Total Owner Doctor Compensation	$	**188,310**
Amortization		0
Depreciation		15,994
Interest Expense		0
Total Other Expenses	$	**204,304**
NET OTHER INCOME	$	**(204,190)**
NET INCOME	$	**208,588**

APPENDIX 3
IMPORTANT NUMBERS WORKSHEET

▷ **BALANCE SHEET-RELATED**

Cash on Hand _____

Long-Term Debt _____

Distributions _____

Tax Basis/Equity _____

▷ **PROFIT AND LOSS STATEMENT-RELATED**

Total Income _____

Net Income _____

Owner's Compensation

    Owner's Salary _____

    Owner's Payroll Taxes _____

    Children's Salaries _____

    Children's Payroll Taxes _____

    Health Insurance _____

    Total = _____

Interest Expense _____

Taxes _____

Depreciation _____

Amortization _____

Team Expenses

    Staff Payroll _____

    Contract Labor _____

    Staff Insurance _____

EBITDA

Retirement _____

Staff Payroll Taxes _____

Payroll Processing _____

Uniforms and Laundry _____

Staff Recruitment _____

Total Team Expenses = _____

Facilities

Rent _____

Repairs and Maintenance _____

Utilities _____

Total Facilities = _____

Dental Supplies _____

Lab Expenses _____

Marketing _____

Office Supplies and Expense _____

Associate Compensation

Salary _____

Payroll Taxes _____

Health Insurance _____

Other Benefits _____

Total Associate Compensation = _____

APPENDIX 4
LIMITED FINANCIAL EXAM WORKSHEET

▷ **OWNER'S COMPENSATION**

Personal Distributions _____

W-2 Wages _____

Doctor Payroll Taxes _____

Health Insurance _____

Family Wages _____

Family Payroll Taxes _____

Retirement _____

TOTAL OWNER'S COMPENSATION _____

▷ **TAX RESERVES**

Tax Distributions _____

Non-Payroll Taxes from P&L _____

TOTAL TAX RESERVES _____

▷ **OVERHEAD**

Total Expenses from P&L _____

Plus (+) Debt Payments _____

    New Expense Total _____

Subtract (-) Previously Considered

    Doctor W-2 Wages _____

    Doctor Payroll Taxes _____

    Other Doctor Benefits _____

Taxes _____

Interest Expense _____

Depreciation _____

Amortization _____

TOTAL OVERHEAD _____

▷ **PROFIT** _____

Total Income _____

Subtract (-)

Owner's Compensation _____

Tax Reserves _____

Overhead _____

TOTAL PROFIT _____

ENDNOTES

[1] Julie C. Swift, Terry D. Rees, Jacqueline M. Plemons, William W. Hallmon and John C. Wright, "The Effectiveness of 1% Pimecrolimus Cream in the Treatment of Oral Erosive Lichen Planus," *Journal of Periodontology*, April 2005/Vol. 76, Issue 4, p. 627-635.

[2] Dave Ramsey, *The Total Money Makeover* (Nashville, TN: Thomas Nelson, 2013).

[3] Mike Michalowicz, *Profit First: Transform Your Business From a Cash-Eating Monster to a Money-Making Machine* (New York, NY: Portfolio Penguin, 2014).

[4] Cecelia M. Ford, PhD, "Toni Morrison: The Power of Fiction in the Arc of Progress," Women's Voices for Change, June 4, 2020, https://womensvoicesforchange.org/toni-morrison-the-power-of-fiction-in-the-arc-of-progress.htm, accessed April 23, 2023.

[5] Dr. Julie Woods, Mike Michalowicz, and Ron Saharyan, "Episode 324: Dr. Julie Woods: Journey to Becoming a Financially Literate Business Owner," Grow My Accounting Practice Podcast, September 9, 2021, https://growmyaccountingpractice.libsyn.com/gmap-ep-324, accessed April 23, 2023.

[6] Julie Woods and Chris Sands, "Episode 3: Stuff People Ask" Pro-FI 20/20, CPAs YouTube channel, June 16, 2021, https://www.youtube.com/watch?v=_rJnWuCvYAw, accessed April 23, 2023.

[7] Alice Calaprice, ed., *The Ultimate Quotable Einstein*, (Princeton, New Jersey: Princeton University Press, 2010) "Misattributed to Einstein" section, 474.

[8] Michael E. Gerber, Dr. Alan Kwong Hing, and Christopher Barrow, *The E-Myth Dentist* (Carlsbad, CA: Prodigy Business Books, Inc., 2013).

[9] Gerber, Kwong Hing, and Barrow, *The E-Myth Dentist*

[10] Definition of "salary." Merriam-Webster.com, https://www.merriam-

webster.com/dictionary/salary, accessed April 23, 2023.

[11] Greg Crabtree with Beverly Blair Harzog, *Simple Numbers, Straight Talk, Big Profits!* (Huntsville, AL: MJ Lane Publishing, 2011).

[12] Definition of "profit." Merriam-Webster.com, https://www.merriam-webster.com/dictionary/profit, accessed April 23, 2023.

[13] Michalowicz, *Profit First*

[14] Melissa Houston, "How This Cash Collector Turns Outdated Accounts into Cash Quickly," Forbes.com, https://www.forbes.com/sites/melissahouston/2020/12/22/how-this-cash-collector-turns-outdated-accounts-into-cash-quickly/?sh=76cb6fadd7a3, accessed April 23, 2023.

[15] Donna Kelley, Slavica Singer, and Mike Herrington, "Global Entrepreneurship Monitor 2015/16 Global Report," Global Entrepreneurship Monitor, February 5, 2016, https://www.gemconsortium.org/report/gem-2015-2016-global-report, accessed April 23, 2023.

[16] Crabtree, *Simple Numbers*

[17] Crabtree, *Simple Numbers*

[18] Crabtree, *Simple Numbers*

[19] *Jerry Maguire*, directed by Cameron Crowe (produced by Gracie Films, distributed by TriStar Pictures, 1996), https://en.wikipedia.org/wiki/Jerry_Maguire, accessed April 23, 2023.

[20] Michalowicz, *Profit First*

[21] Michalowicz, *Profit First*

[22] "Comparison is the thief of joy" quote, Quote Investigator, https://quoteinvestigator.com/2021/02/06/thief-of-joy/, accessed April 23, 2023.

[23] Gerber, Kwong Hing, and Barrow, *The E-Myth Dentist*

[24] Mike Michalowicz, *Get Different: Marketing that Can't Be Ignored!* (New York, NY: Penguin, 2021).

[25] "Employee Theft No Longer an If—Now It Is How Much," Law Firm Newswire, April 19, 2013, https://lawfirmnewswire.com/2013/04/employee-theft-no-longer-an-if-now-it-is-how-much/#:~:text=New%20

Kessler%20Survey%20finds%20that%2095%25%20of%20
employees,employers%2C%20up%20from%2079%25%20in%20
Kessler's%201999%20study, accessed April 23, 2023.

26 Michalowicz, *Profit First*

27 Ramsey, *Total Money Makeover*

28 The Budget Mom: https://www.thebudgetmom.com, accessed April 23, 2023.

29 Michalowicz, *Profit First*

30 Nat Eliason, "Parkinson's Law Isn't Just About Time," author blog, November 29, 2015, https://www.nateliason.com/blog/parkinsons-law-isnt-just-about-time, accessed April 23, 2023.

31 Michalowicz, *Profit First*

32 Michalowicz, *Profit First*

33 Definition of "primacy effect." Primary Effect: Meaning, How It Works (verywellmind.com), accessed April 30, 2023.

34 William Hiltz, Hiltz & Associates: Hiltz & Associates | Dentistry's Embezzlement & Forensic Data Experts (hiltzandassociates.com), accessed April 30, 2023.

35 Mike Michalowicz, *The Pumpkin Plan: A Simple Strategy to Grow a Remarkable Business in Any Field* (New York, NY: Penguin, 2012).

36 Atul Gawande, *The Checklist Manifesto* (New York, NY: Metropolitan Books, 2009).

37 Gerber, Kwong Hing, and Barrow, *The E-Myth Dentist*

38 Gerber, Kwong Hing, and Barrow, *The E-Myth Dentist*

39 Dr. Stephanie Mapp, Mapp Your Practice: https://mappyourpractice.com, accessed April 23, 2023.

40 William Hiltz, Hiltz & Associates: Hiltz & Associates | Dentistry's Embezzlement & Forensic Data Experts (hiltzandassociates.com), accessed April 30, 2023.

[41] Collier, Sarner & Associates (now Collier & Associates, Inc.): https://www.collieradvisors.com, accessed April 23, 2023.

[42] Ramsey Solutions, "How the Debt Snowball Method Works," https://www.ramseysolutions.com/debt/how-the-debt-snowball-method-works, accessed April 23, 2023.

[43] Michalowicz, *Profit First*

[44] Greg Martin, The Entrepreneur's Banker: http://www.GPM-financial.com, accessed April 23, 2023.

[45] DiSC™ Profile: https://www.discprofile.com, accessed April 23, 2023.

[46] William Moulton Marston, *Emotions of Normal People* (Taylor & Francis, Ltd., Oxfordshire, England, UK, 1928).

[47] Dr. Teresa M. Scott: https://holisticdentalassociates.com/meet-your-dental-team/, accessed April 30, 2023.

[48] U.S. Equal Employment Opportunity Commission, "[EEOC] Recordkeeping Requirements," https://www.eeoc.gov/employers/recordkeeping-requirements, accessed April 23, 2023.

[49] AJ Harper, *Write A Must-Read* (Vancouver, BC, Canada: Page Two, 2022).

[50] Vantage Circle, "91 Best Quotes For Training Employees," August 1, 2022, https://blog.vantagecircle.com/quotes-for-training-employees/, accessed April 23, 2023.

[51] Vantage Circle, "91 Best Quotes"

[52] Upstream Dental Coaching: https://upstreamdentalcoaching.com/, accessed April 30, 2023.

[53] Cornell Law School Legal Information Institute, "26 U.S. Code § 280A - Disallowance of certain expenses in connection with business use of home, rental of vacation homes, etc.," https://www.law.cornell.edu/uscode/text/26/280A, accessed April 23, 2023.

[54] Arthur C. Brooks, *From Strength to Strength* (New York, NY: Penguin, 2022).

[55] "Should I Stay or Should I Go," The Clash, from *Combat Rock*, CBS Records, 1982. YouTube: https://www.youtube.com/

watch?v=BN1WwnEDWAM, accessed April 23, 2023.

[56] Dr. Josie Dovidio, Yoga for Dentists: https://yogafordentists.net, accessed April 23, 2023.

[57] Whitney Goodman, *Toxic Positivity* (New York, NY: Penguin, 2022).

[58] Saul Mcleod, PhD, "SRRS—Stressful Life Events and Daily Hassles," Simply Psychology, updated April 21, 2023, https://www.simplypsychology.org/SRRS.html, accessed April 23, 2023.

[59] Dr. Josie Dovidio, Yoga for Dentists: https://yogafordentists.net, accessed April 23, 2023.

[60] *14 Peaks: Nothing Is Impossible,* directed by Torquil Jones (Netflix, 2022), https://www.netflix.com/title/81464765, accessed April 23, 2023.

ACKNOWLEDGMENTS

WHEN I WAS DATING MY husband Brad, I told him, "If I ever tell you I'm hungry, that means I am *very* hungry, and I probably should have eaten thirty minutes ago." He took that message to heart and has always tried to make sure I have what I need. He had to pick up the slack for me numerous times while I was writing this book. Not only did he not complain when I took over our dining room table or took my laptop on vacation, he even made sure I had snacks when I couldn't break my concentration long enough to pause and enjoy happy hour. Without his sacrifices, encouragement, and willingness to share some of our story, this book would not be in your hands.

The book is dedicated to my daughter Rachel. I hit the jackpot with her. I am thrilled that she is considering a career in dentistry, especially since it is because of the lifestyle and balance I have as a working mom. No matter what she chooses to study after high school, she will thrive, and I'm thankful she is kind.

My parents, Ellen and Walter Horn, have selflessly given me unconditional love and support my whole life. Without that, I wouldn't be the person I am today.

I must thank Mike Michalowicz for giving me the tools I needed to turn my business around and inspiring me to share my own story.

This book wouldn't be as reader-focused without the input and mentorship of AJ Harper (who helped write *Profit First*).

Additionally, she created a safe place for aspiring authors to learn and support each other and I'm glad to be an active participant. Special shout-out to Laura Stone, who helped keep me organized, accountable, and feeling more confident in my progress thanks to her guidance and generous use of pom-poms and praise.

To my dental colleagues who tried the exercises for "doability" and the advance readers who gave honest feedback on an early draft of this book: I appreciate you more than you could know ... unless you write your own book someday. You are true trailblazers!

ABOUT THE AUTHOR

In 2020, Dr. Julie C. Woods became a certified Profit First Professional, the first and only dentist to do so. Dr. Woods helps colleagues understand their businesses and increase their profitability by analyzing their practice numbers and helping them successfully implement the Profit First cash management system. Dr. Woods has been a practicing periodontist since finishing her residency at Baylor University in 2004. When she isn't eating and drinking her way across the globe, she lives with her husband and daughter in Topeka, Kansas.

9 798987 540213